The Breakfast Cereal Gourmet

THE BREAKFAST CEREAL

Gourmet

DAVID HOFFMAN

Andrews McMeel
Publishing
Kansas City

05 06 07 08 09 WKT 10 9 8 7 6 5 4 3 2 1

Library of Congress Cataloging-in Publication Data
Hoffman, David, 1953–
    The breakfast cereal gourmet / David Hoffman.
        p. cm.
    ISBN 0-7407-5029-1
        1. Cookery (Cereal) 2. Cookery, American. 3. Cereals, Prepared—Miscellanea.
    I. Title.

TX808.H64 2005
641.6'31—dc22

2004062721

Book design and composition by Holly Camerlinck

Attention: Schools and Businesses
Andrews McMeel books are available at quantity discounts with bulk purchase for
educational, business, or sales promotional use. For information, please write to:
Special Sales Department, Andrews McMeel Publishing, 4520 Main Street, Kansas City,
Missouri 64111.

CONTENTS

INTRODUCTION

In 1997 I received a phone call from a software company who, riding high on the success of a smart, hip, best-selling CD-ROM, wanted to know if I was available—and interested—in helping them to develop their next big thing. To be truthful, the offer surprised me. I'd spent the bulk of my career writing books and scripts and working as a television reporter, none of which had particularly prepared me for a ride on the information superhighway. But two weeks later I found myself in their offices, a forty-three-year-old surrounded by a sea of twenty-something Alpha Geeks, Stress Puppies, and Ivy League–educated dot-commers, whose conversations were peppered with buzzwords like *applications, shareware,* and *system requirements.* It is an image that, through the years, stayed with me. Funny thing is, the memory has nothing to do with anything that came out of their mouths during those five days—and everything to do with what went into them.

Cereal.

Lots and lots of brightly colored, sugarcoated breakfast cereal. So much cereal, in fact, that the office kitchen was stocked with nothing but. We're talking Cinnamon Toast Crunch, Cocoa Puffs, Cocoa Krispies, Cookie Crisp, Quisp, Froot Loops, Fruity Pebbles, Frosted Flakes . . . and that was just the top shelf.

Shortly thereafter I read about an engaged couple in San Francisco who had picked out a pair of $200 Waterford dishes and listed them on their wedding gift registry as "His and Hers Cereal Bowls." On a trip to New York, I discovered that at his shop under the Brooklyn Bridge (and now at his Chocolate Haven in lower Manhattan), Food Network personality (and former Le Cirque pastry chef) Jacque Torres was offering Chocolate-Covered Corn Flakes at $20 per pound (a side note: they're amazing). And then I heard that Arizona State University in Tempe was home to Cereality, the first in a proposed nationwide chain of cereal "bars" (think Starbucks meets Ben & Jerry's) where the menu features a choice of 33 name brands, 34 toppings, and 8 different milks—prepared and served by a staff who are dressed in their pajamas.

Suddenly, everywhere I turned, cold cereal was hot.

As a baby boomer, I understood the appeal. After all, cereal is comfort food—ranking up there with meat loaf or macaroni and cheese. It is also retro nostalgia, a reminder of Howdy Doody, Soupy Sales, and the freedom of Saturday mornings in front of the TV. But for the generation who followed me, it is all that and much, much more. Cereal is no longer just a food—it is a food group.

Which got me to thinking: If people are now eating cereal for breakfast, lunch, and supper (not to mention as an appetizer, side dish, or dessert), why not a book that celebrates this obsession? A combination of history and how-to that, with the help of some very famous chefs, takes cereal out of the bowl and puts it front and center on the dining room table.

Cap'n Crunch Crab Cakes, anyone?

The Breakfast Cereal Gourmet

A HEALTHY START

1830s

Dr. Sylvester Graham, a Pennsylvania Presbyterian minister (not an MD), appalled by the pork-and-beef heavy English-style breakfasts most Americans are eating, preaches the value of vegetarianism and good nutrition (and the evils of alcohol and caffeine) and in the process develops Graham flour and Graham crackers.

1863

Dr. James Jackson of Dansville, New York, purchases large quantities of Graham flour, bakes them in large sheets, then breaks them up, rebakes them, and breaks them up again to create a breakfast product that he names Granula.

1894

William Keith Kellogg, brother to John and a manager at the San, attempts to salvage a batch of stale wheatmeal by grinding it. He discovers that when it is run through rollers, the wheat—rather than coming out as a unified flat sheet—comes out as flakes. He roasts the flakes and serves them to his patients, who can't get enough of the new menu offering known as Granose. Several years later, Kellogg would repeat the same process using corn. Unable to convince John (who felt that blatant commerical ventures would compromise his integrity as a medical professional) that they should, like Post, sell their discoveries to grocery stores, he buys out his brother's share of the patents, forms the Kellogg Company, and in 1902 begins mass production of his first cereal. Foregoing any name that sounds too medicinal, he decides to simply call the product Corn Flakes.

1887

Dr. John Harvey Kellogg, a follower of Graham's, Seventh Day Adventist and director of the Battle Creek Sanitarium ("The San") in Battle Creek, Michigan, also develops a morning mix of baked and rebaked grains, and also calls it Granula. Word of his great new food item travels quickly, and—surprise, surprise—he is sued by Dr. Jackson. So Kellogg changes the name of his product to Granola. But slow down: While Granola is a menu staple at the sanitarium, Kellogg turns his attention to nuts, and never bothers to market the cereal.

1891

Enter Charles W. Post, a patient at the San, who leaves uncured, decides to opens his own health retreat, and concocts his own "easier-to-chew" version of Kellogg's Granola recipe. He does sell it commercially (thus making his mix the first packaged cold cereal product)—and quite successfully—under the name Grape Nuts.

POSTSCRIPT:
· · · · · · · · ·

Some historians say that the birth of breakfast cereal in America actually pre-dates Granula, Granola, Granose, and Grape Nuts by at least a hundred years—citing that colonial housewives frequently served popcorn, sprinkled with sugar and doused in cream, as a morning meal. But for most of us, what came first is inconsequential. As we see it, breakfast wasn't worth a grain until 1949, when Sugar Crisp, the first sweetened cereal, was introduced . . . and the mid-1950s, when the industry began advertising on TV.

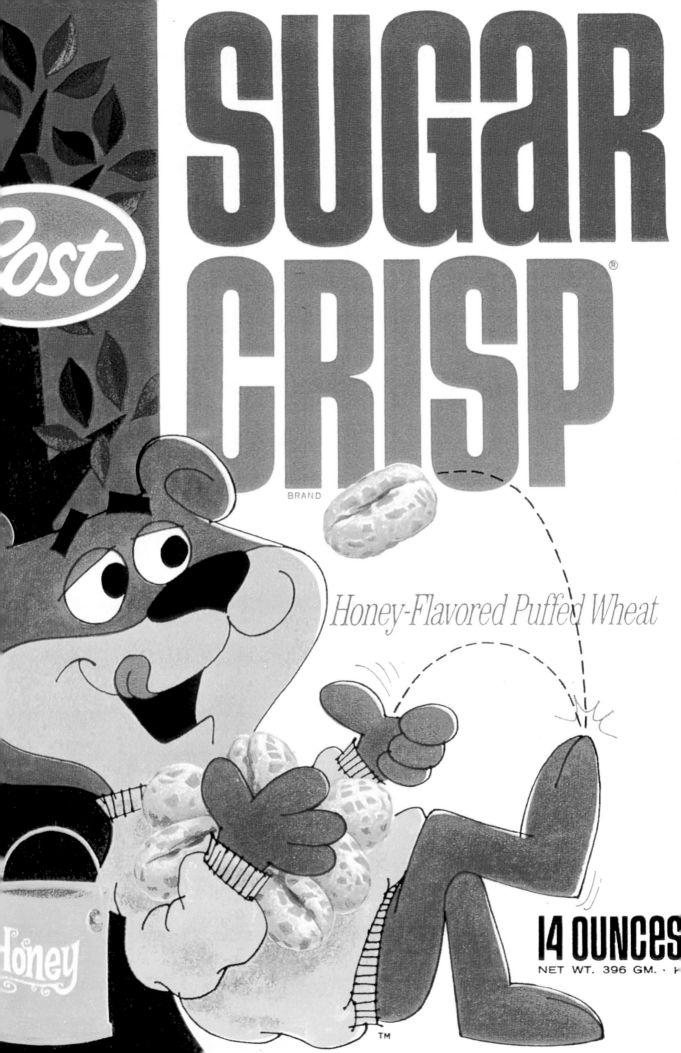

(SNAP, CRACKLE)
POP GOES THE CULTURE

On any given day, one out of every two Americans starts the morning with a bowl of cereal.

The average person consumes about ten pounds—or 160 bowls of cereal—per year.

Breakfast cereals rank third in the list of grocery store items on which Americans spend their money, behind carbonated beverages and milk—and ahead of bread, hamburger, and cigarettes.

The U.S. cereal industry uses in excess of 800 million pounds of sugar per year, enough to coat every person with more than three pounds of sugar.

The cereal with the highest amount of sugar is Honey Smacks, at almost 56 percent.

There are more than four hundred brands of ready-to-eat breakfast cereals on America's supermarket shelves.

Most of the vitamins and minerals kids get come from breakfast cereals.

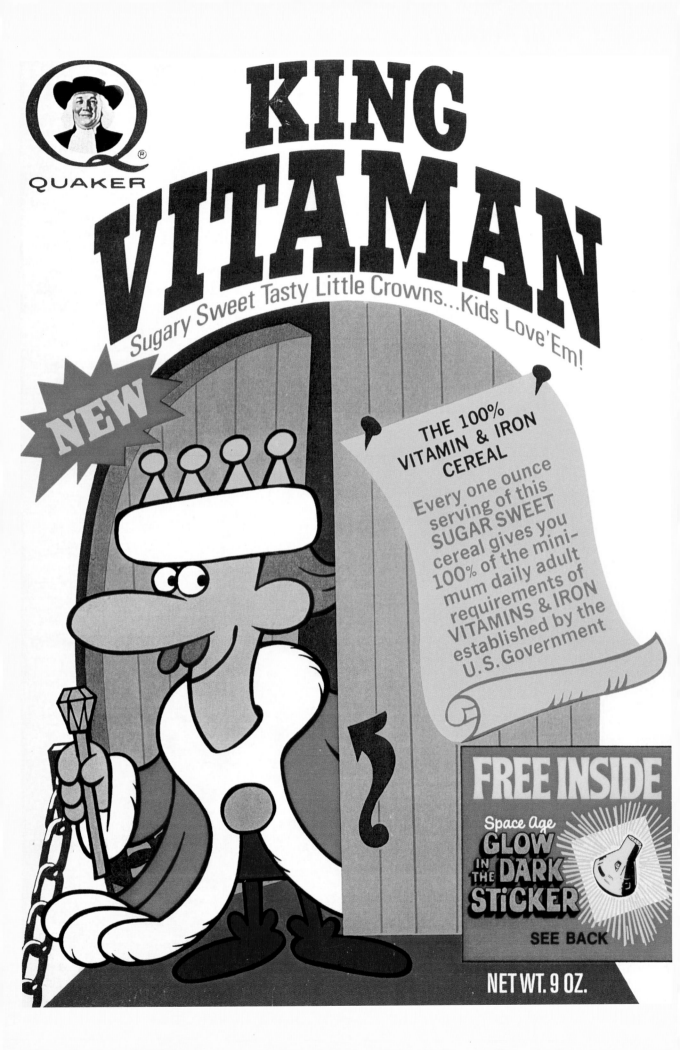

Many cereal companies add iron to their products to make them more nutritious. Ever wonder what—exactly—this iron looks like?

Grab some fortified cereal (any brand will do), a bowl, a spoon . . . and a MAGNET. Then try this:

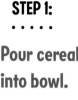

STEP 1:
· · · · ·

Pour cereal into bowl.

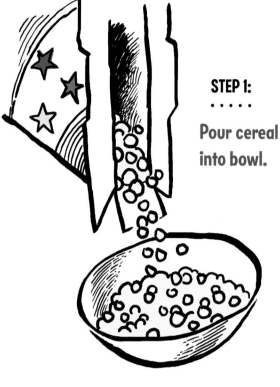

STEP 2:
· · · · ·

Mash it with a spoon (or other utensil). The more finely ground the cereal, the better.

crunch crunch crunch

STEP 3:
· · · · ·

Stir the magnet through the crushed cereal.

STEP 4:
· · · · ·

Pull the magnet out. The black fuzz you see? That's iron.

The first registered trademarked cereal character was the Quaker Man ("Nothing is better for thee than me") in 1877.

The Chicago waiter who posed for the portrait of Rastus, the chef featured on the front of the Cream of Wheat package, received a one-time payment of five dollars (roughly $200 by today's economic standards). He might have been rewarded more—but the company never heard from him again.

· · · · · · · · · · · · · · · ·

While working for Post cereals in product development, Al Clausi drew on his background as an Italian American and figured if pasta could be manufactured in a myriad of shapes then a macaroni extruder could also be used to produce a novelty cereal, one that went beyond the normal flakes, puffs, shreds, and O's. The result? Alpha-Bits.

Cereal characters don't always directly relate to the product they're fronting, but in a clever turn, the mid-1960s boxes of Alpha-Bits featured Loveable Truly, a mail carrier who delivered "letters."

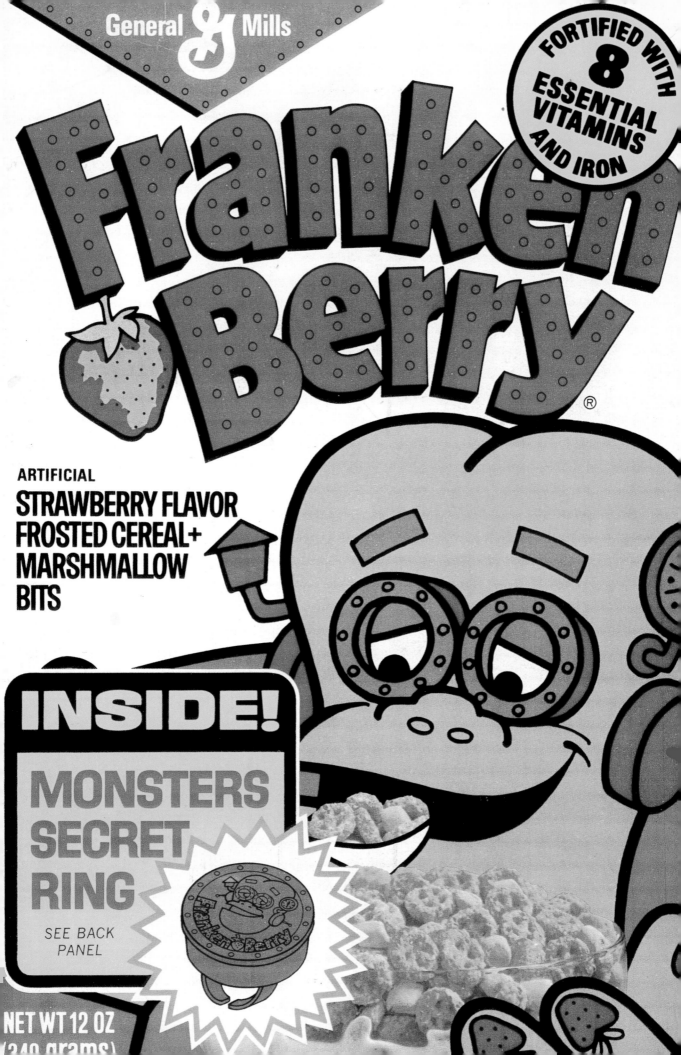

Soon after launching Franken Berry in 1971, General Mills was forced to recall the product and pull it from supermarket shelves. Seems that after eating it, when kids went to the bathroom, their poop had turned pink from the food coloring.

. . . .

More than 1.3 million cereal commercials air on American television yearly. Only automobile manufacturers spend more money advertising on TV.

Struggling to create a new ad campaign for Kellogg's Raisin Bran in the late 1960s, ad exec Danny Nichols took a box of the product home, then spent the evening analyzing it, trying to single out those qualities that separated this brand from the pack. As a matter of course, he dumped the contents onto his kitchen table and began to play with them. Grabbing a miniature scoop he used to measure out coffee, he filled it with raisins. Twice. The next day, when asked by his agency if he had come up with anything, he informed them that he had.

"There are two scoops of raisins in every box," he announced.

Kellogg's
RAISIN
BRAN
NOW WITH SUGAR
FROSTED RAISINS
SEE PACKAGE BACK
FOR ANOTHER
SUN FUN
GAME!
NET WT. 14 OZ.

"Today yore vittle money fetches more than ever before"

Since the 1950s, a slew of famous faces have been used to sell breakfast cereal, in particular TV cowboys and Saturday-morning regulars like Yogi Bear, Huckleberry Hound, Fred and Barney, and Rocky and Bullwinkle. In the 1960s, sitcom stars (like Elizabeth Montgomery of *Bewitched* and Jay North of *Dennis the Menace*) and show casts (*The Monkees, The Partridge Family, The Beverly Hillbillies*) joined their ranks, appearing (in character) in print ads and on-air spots touting the brands that sponsored their popular series.

Sci-fi writer Neal Stephenson's *Cryptonomicon* includes a multipage treatise on eating Cap'n Crunch; in paragraph after paragraph, the author waxes passionate over the physical properties of its pillowlike kernels. It's a fact not lost on the Blue Man Group, whose long running off-Broadway (and worldwide) theatrical hit includes a Cap'n Crunch Symphony where the trio turns the cereal into a percussion instrument—chewing and consuming it in synchronicity, to the accompaniment of a live band.

. . . .

1970s aficionado Quentin Tarantino repeatedly—and prominently—features vintage cereals of that decade in his films: Check Mr. Orange's (Tim Roth's) apartment in *Reservoir Dogs* for a box of Fruit Brute; Lance (Eric Stoltz) is seen eating the same cereal in *Pulp Fiction*; and in *Kill Bill Vol. 1*, Vernita Green (Vivica A. Fox) takes a gun out of a box of Kaboom (get it?), in an ill-fated attempt to blow away the Bride (played by Uma Thurman).

General Mills

HIGH NUTRITION CEREAL

KABOOM®

A TOASTED OAT CEREAL WITH MARSHMALLOW STARS

NET WT 9 OZ (255 grams)

DICK DETZNER raised some eyebrows—and delighted critics—when his painting *The Last Pancake Breakfast* appeared in 2001 at the Chicago Athenaeum: Museum of Architecture and Design. A satire of *The Last Supper,* the work gives a whole new interpretation to *The Da Vinci Code*; it puts Mrs. Butterworth front and center and Cap'n Crunch with a spilled glass (in this case, it's orange juice) at his plate. **LIZA LOU**'s life-size glass-bead-covered environments have been mounted at the Smithsonian as well as the New Museum in New York; her 168-square-foot installation known as *The Kitchen* features a breakfast table covered with artful renditions of boxes and half-eaten bowls of cereal, including Trix and Frosted Flakes. And **BURTON MORRIS**, whose signature style put a bold graphic face on the 76th Academy Awards and the 2004 Summer Olympic Games, has produced a series of eight acrylic-on-canvas cereal boxes, turning pop culture into Pop Art—at $3,200 a pop.

· · · · · · · · · · · · · · · · ·

Vintage cereal boxes, particularly those from the 1950s, '60s, and '70s, have become highly collectible, commonly commanding prices between $200 and $300—and up. Some early packages of Quisp (before he lost his politically incorrect ray gun) and Quake (before the burly miner was transformed into an urban cowboy) can fetch as much as $800. But it's either the 1970 Nabisco Wheat Honeys or 1970 Nabisco Rice Honeys—the one featuring a Beatles sticker and their Yellow Submarine on the front—that is the collector's holy grail, and could, according to those who know, bring up to $2,000.

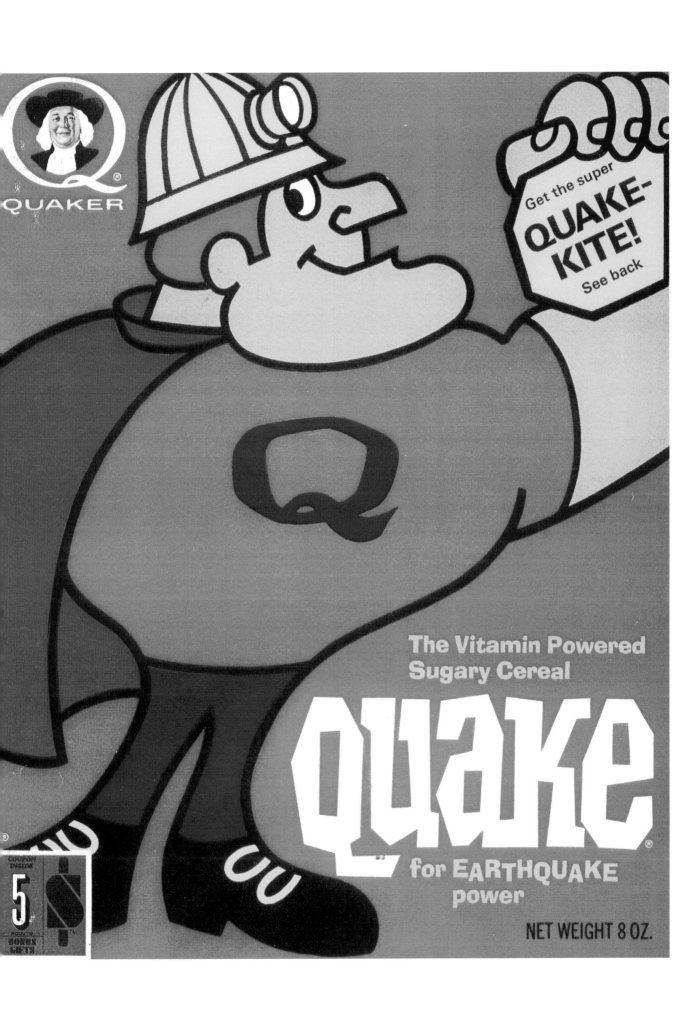

THINKING OUTSIDE THE BOX

While entrées made from flakes or puffs would crop up on the menu at the Battle Creek Sanitarium in the late 1800s (more Bran Loaf with Mayonnaise Dressing, please!), it took over forty years—and a home economics graduate from Iowa State—to put cooking with cereal on the mainstream culinary map.

In 1939, Mildred Day, who worked for Kellogg's, decided to use one of the company's products to develop a snack. Ironically, she didn't do it as part of her job or even for her employer, but rather, because she and a friend, Malitta Jensen, had been asked to create something to be sold as a fund-raiser for a group of Camp Fire Girls. Inspired by the popcorn balls found on boardwalks and at county fairs, the two women varied that formula; they replaced popped corn with puffed rice (in the form of Rice Krispies), then combined that with butter, vanilla, and (instead of corn syrup) the signature campfire sweet—marshmallows. Their "Crispy Squares" (later to be called "Marshmallow Treats" before being trademarked "Rice Krispies Treats") proved so popular that by 1941, Kellogg's had started printing the recipe on all of the product's packages.

Howdy Doody's Favorite Treat...
9-Minute
MARSHMALLOW "CRISPY SQUARES"

Say, Mom! Why not make some for the kids—or let _them_ make 'em ... it's that easy. Just Rice Krispies and Marshmallows. And good? Oh, Boy!

© KAGRAN

RECIPE ON EVERY PACKAGE

The wonderful thing about what you see here is _not_ just how _good_ Marshmallow Crispy Squares look and taste. No, ma'am. It's how downright _easy_ they are to make. Take a look at the recipe below. Now compare it with what's on the plate. See what we mean? All it takes to get this same result in your kitchen is Kellogg's Rice Krispies (a cereal you should have on hand anyway), some marshmallows, and nine minutes. For Halloween "trick or treat"—or tonight, for that matter. How about it?

9-MINUTE MARSHMALLOW "CRISPY SQUARES"

¼ cup butter or margarine
½ pound marshmallows (about 2½ dozen)
5 cups of Kellogg's Rice Krispies
½ teaspoon vanilla

1. Cook butter and marshmallows over boiling water until syrupy, stirring frequently.

2. Add vanilla; beat thoroughly.

3. Put Rice Krispies in greased large bowl and pour on marshmallow mixture, stirring briskly.

4. Press into greased shallow pan; cut into squares when cool. Yield: 24 squares, about 2 inches each (13 x 9-inch pan).

Kellogg's

THEY'RE SWEET ON EACH OTHER; THEY'RE AT YOUR GROCER'S NOW

RICE KRISPIES and MARSHMALLOWS

The rationale behind any recipe that includes cold cereal as an ingredient breaks down to one thing: mouth feel. Its inherent crunchiness makes it ideal as the base of a coating, crust, topping, layer, stuffing, or binder. The general rule of thumb? Crushed or ground, cereal works great in tandem with—or as a substitution for—flour, bread crumbs, nuts, or cornmeal. From there, it's a matter of personal preference. But two guarantees: Cooking with cereal will give food great texture (and even opting for a flake, say, over a puff, a crisp, or an "O" can make a subtle difference) and cooking with cereal will tweak food's taste in surprising ways (depending on whether the grain you choose is corn, wheat, rice, oat, or bran—and whether or not it's been sweetened).

Ready. Set. Pour.

CORN FLAKE-CRUSTED FISH FILLETS WITH ROASTED TOMATILLO SAUCE AND FRIED CORN

James Beard Award–winner **RICK BAYLESS** is the chef-proprietor of Chicago's hugely successful Frontera Grill and its elegant neighbor, Topolobampo, where this multitextured dish (known as Pescado Encornflecado en Verde con Esquites Fritos) is a favorite on the menu.

Taking the concept of corn flakes fried chicken—a long-time back-of-the-box-recipe staple—to a nuevo level, it may seem like more than you would want to tackle at home. But Bayless points out you can prepare it in stages. He suggests making the sauce and the corn a day ahead (store them separately, covered, in the refrigerator—then reheat both when ready to use). Similarly, the fish can be breaded up to six hours ahead and fried just prior to serving.

FISH FILLETS

½ cup all-purpose flour
Salt
2 large eggs
One 7-ounce box corn flakes (approximately 7 cups)
Six 6-ounce skinless fish fillets (snapper, grouper, halibut, striped
  bass, mahimahi, or other thickish, medium-flake, light-flavored fish),
  about ¾-inch thick

1. To "bread" the fish, spread the flour into a deep plate (or pie plate), then stir in ½ teaspoon salt. Into another deep plate, break the eggs, and add 3 tablespoons water and ½ teaspoon salt. Beat with a fork until completely liquid. Into a third plate, spread the corn flakes, then use the back of a measuring cup to gently break them into ¼-inch pieces.

2. Dredge all sides of a piece of fish in the flour, then lay it in the egg mixture. Use a large fork to flip it over and carefully transfer the drippy piece of fish to the plate of corn flakes. Sprinkle flakes from the dish over the top of the fish and press them in firmly; the fish should be thoroughly coated with flakes. Transfer to another plate or baking sheet, then repeat with the remaining fillets. Refrigerate uncovered at least 1 hour or up to 6 hours.

SAUCE

· · · · ·

1 pound (10 to 12 medium) tomatillos, husked and rinsed

Fresh hot green chiles to taste (roughly 3 serranos or 1 jalapeño), stemmed

2 tablespoons olive oil

1 medium white onion, sliced

3 large garlic cloves, peeled and finely chopped

2 cups fish or chicken stock

2/3 cup loosely packed chopped fresh cilantro, plus a few sprigs for garnish

1. Roast the tomatillos and chiles on a baking sheet 4 inches below a very hot broiler until darkly roasted, even blackened in spots, about 5 minutes. Flip them over and roast the other side—4 or 5 minutes more will give you splotchy-black and blistered tomatillos and chiles that are soft and cooked through. Cool and transfer everything to a food processor or blender, being careful to scrape up all the delicious juice that has run out onto the baking sheet. Process until smoothly pureed.

2. Set a 4-quart heavy saucepan over medium heat and measure in 1 tablespoon of the olive oil. When hot, add the onion and cook, stirring regularly, until richly golden, about 7 minutes. Stir in the garlic and cook a minute longer.

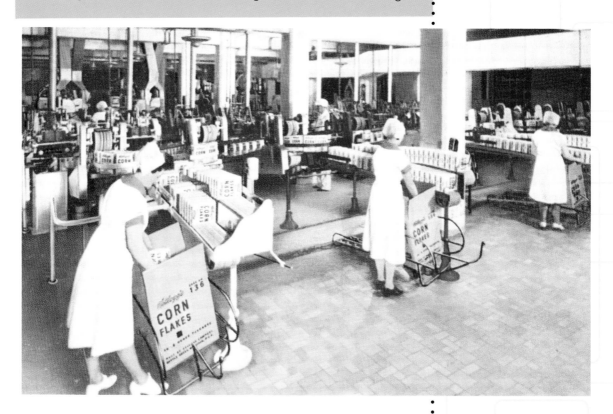

3. Raise the heat to medium-high, and, when really sizzling, add the tomatillo puree all at once. Stir until noticeably darker and very thick, 3 or 4 minutes. Add the broth and ⅓ cup of the cilantro. Stir everything thoroughly. Simmer, stirring often, over medium-low heat, until the flavors mellow and the consistency thickens enough to coat a spoon (but not too heavily), about 30 minutes. Taste and season with salt, usually about ¾ teaspoon. Keep warm over low heat. Thin with a bit of water if it is too thick.

GRILLED CORN

2 cups fresh corn kernels (about 3 ears of sweet corn, or 2 ears of field corn)

In a medium-size skillet, heat the remaining 1 tablespoon of olive oil over medium. When hot, add the corn and stir frequently until nicely browned, 5 to 10 minutes. Sweet corn will be a little chewy, field corn will be quite chewy, meaning you may want to dribble a little water in the pan to steam the kernels to a bit more tenderness. Remove the pan from the heat and set aside.

TO FINISH

Vegetable oil to a depth of ¼ inch for pan-frying the fish

1. While heating ¼ inch of vegetable oil in a large, heavy skillet over medium to medium-high, turn on the oven to its lowest setting. When the oil is hot enough to make an edge of a "breaded" fillet really sizzle, fry the fillets in two batches. (They shouldn't be crowded in the pan or they won't crust and brown nicely.) They'll need to cook about 2 minutes per side to brown and be done enough to flake under firm pressure—it takes a little practice to check this without breaking the crust very much. Carefully transfer the cooked fillets to a paper towel-lined baking sheet and keep warm in the low oven while you're frying the second batch.

2. Spoon the warm sauce (thin it with water if it has thickened) onto a deep warm platter and arrange the crusty fish fillets slightly overlapping down the center. Sprinkle the whole affair with the corn (reheat it if it has cooled off) and the remaining ⅓ cup of cilantro. Now you're ready to make your triumphant entrance to the dining room.

 Serves 6

BAKED MACARONI AND CHEESE

After doing culinary time in the kitchens of noted Los Angeles institutions like Campanile, Spago, and La Brea Bakery, **ANNIE MILER** opened Clementine, one of those quintessential neighborhood restaurants where her "homemade seasonal food"—roasted tomato soup, old-fashioned oatmeal, deviled eggs, and the world's best chocolate pudding—makes you wish you lived in the neighborhood. Miler's signature macaroni and cheese ("I don't know of many recipes that call for Velveeta and crème fraîche, but I do recommend crème fraîche over sour cream because it will not curdle when you bake it") has the perfect crunch—thanks to a heaping of crushed Kellogg's Corn Flakes baked on top.

CASEROLE

3¾ cups whole milk
3 tablespoons butter
3 tablespoons all-purpose flour
3 ounces gruyére cheese, grated
3 ounces sharp cheddar cheese, grated
6 ounces Velveeta cut in 1-inch cubes
½ cup crème fraîche
½ teaspoon Worcestershire sauce
Pinch of cayenne
Salt and black pepper to taste
1 pound elbow macaroni, cooked al dente

1. In a small saucepan, heat the milk just to the boiling point.

2. In a separate medium saucepan, melt the 3 tablespoons butter, then add the flour, stirring constantly. The mixture should bubble but not brown. Continue to cook for 2 to 3 minutes over medium-low heat. Add the hot milk, gradually, whisking vigorously to prevent lumps, and let the mixture cook for an additional 5 minutes. Reduce the heat, then add the cheeses and Velveeta, gently stirring until smooth. Remove from the heat.

3. Preheat the oven to 375 degrees.

4. To the mixture in pan, add the crème fraîche, Worcestershire sauce, cayenne, salt, and pepper; stir to combine. Then add the cooked maca-roni. The mixture will seem really soupy, but that's how it should be—it will become nice and creamy and gooey when you bake it. Pour the mixture into a shallow 2-quart casserole dish.

TOPPING
. . . . . .

1 cup crushed corn flakes (about 2 1/2 cups uncrushed)
2 tablespoons butter, melted

In a small bowl, combine the crushed corn flakes and melted butter.

TO FINISH
. . . .

Top the macaroni mixture with the corn flakes mixture, leaving about a 1/2-inch border around the edge. Bake at 375 degrees for 25 to 30 min-utes or until the topping is golden, and the macaroni is hot and bubbly.

(This casserole can be prepared up to 2 days ahead and stored, unbaked, in the refrigerator. When you're ready to serve, bake uncovered at 375 degrees for 40 to 50 minutes).

☞ Serves 4-6

PAN-FRIED RICOTTA CAKES WITH SHAVED PROSCUITTO AND HERB-ALMOND OIL

CAPRIAL PENCE is the chef and co-owner, along with her husband, John, of Caprial's Bistro in Portland, Oregon. Their popular restaurant has spawned a series of successful books, cooking shows (for public television), and most recently, a culinary school. A warning: Not only are these ricotta cakes a savory turn on a classic sweet treat, they're so addicting that you could forget you once liked Rice Krispies mixed with marshmallows.

RICOTTA CAKES

2 ½ cup whole-milk ricotta

½ cup finely ground Parmesan cheese

2 ½ cup finely ground Rice Krispies

2 cloves garlic, finely chopped

4 egg yolks

Salt and black pepper

2 tablespoons extra-virgin olive oil

4 ounces finely sliced proscuitto

1. In a large bowl, place the ricotta, Parmesan cheese, ½ cup of the Rice Krispies, and garlic and mix well. Add the egg yolks and season to taste. Form into 6 equal patties and dredge in remaining Rice Krispies. Chill until ready to use.

2. Julienne the proscuitto and refrigerate until ready to use. Reserve the olive oil until time to finish the dish.

Kellogg's
RICE KRISPIES

Snap!

Crackle!

Pop!

LARGE SIZE—9½ OUNCES NET WT.

OVEN TOASTED RICE WITH SUGAR, SALT, AND MALT FLAVORING. VITAMIN B₁, NIACINAMIDE, AND IRON ADDED

1 oz. provides these percentages of minimum daily adult requirements: Vitamin B₁
11%, Riboflavin 0.45%, Calcium 1%, Phosphorus 4.3%, Iron 5% and 2.0 mg. Niacin.

MADE BY KELLOGG COMPANY, BATTLE CREEK, MICHIGAN, U.S.A.

HERB-ALMOND OIL

½ cup extra-virgin olive oil
2 tablespoons chopped fresh basil
1 teaspoon chopped fresh thyme
2 teaspoons chopped fresh parsley
⅓ cup toasted ground almonds
Sea salt

In a blender or food processor, place the olive oil and herbs, and blend well. Add the almonds and salt, and set aside.

TO FINISH

Heat a very large sauté pan with the reserved 2 tablespoons olive oil until very hot. Add the cakes and cook on each side until golden brown about 5 minutes. Remove the cakes from the pan and place each on a plate. Top with julienned proscuitto and drizzle around the sides with the herb-almond oil. Serve warm.

 Serves 6

During toasting, hot air in the oven causes the kernels of Rice Krispies to expand to several times their original size. As the puffs of rice swell, air pockets are formed. When milk is poured on the cereal these air pockets start to break, causing the distinctive snap-crackle-pop sound.

ASIAN GRILLED CHICKEN SALAD WITH SESAME KRISPS

The Chinese chicken salad—in all its variations—has become a staple on restaurant menus throughout the country, giving classics like the Caesar and the Cobb a run for their money. But the fried wonton strips and crispy rice noodles that lend the dish its signature crunch are not readily available in many markets, making it difficult for the home cook to replicate. Until now.

SESAME KRISPS

- 1 tablespoon light corn syrup
- 1 teaspoon soy sauce
- 2 cups Rice Krispies
- 2 tablespoons toasted sesame seeds

1. Preheat the oven to 200 degrees. Line a baking sheet with lightly oiled foil.

We've just been thru the Kellogg plant where these famous characters put the Snap! Crackle! Pop! in Rice Krispies

2. In a large skillet over medium heat, combine the corn syrup and soy sauce. Add the cereal and toss to coat. Sprinkle with the sesame seeds and toss again. Transfer the mixture to the prepared baking sheet and place in the oven for 5 minutes. Cool slightly, then press with your hands into an even layer. Cool.

DRESSING
• • • • • • •

2 tablespoons sugar
1/2 teaspoon salt
1/2 teaspoon black pepper
1/4 cup rice vinegar
3 tablespoons dark sesame oil
3 tablespoons canola oil

In a small bowl, combine the sugar, salt, pepper, vinegar, and oils. Whisk to blend.

SALAD
• • • • •

6 cups shredded napa cabbage (about 1/2 head)
1/2 cup thinly sliced green onion
1/3 cup toasted slivered almonds
Two 6- to 8-ounce grilled boneless chicken breasts, sliced into strips

In a large bowl, combine the cabbage, onions, almonds, and chicken. Drizzle with the dressing and toss thoroughly. Break the cereal mixture into bite-size pieces. Add to the slaw and toss. Serve immediately.

 Serves 4

CEREAL SAMPLER

(Fresh Raspberry Caramelized Rice Pudding, Peanut Butter-Krispy Cocoa Chewies, and Golden Froot Cupcakes)

GALE GAND is the executive pastry chef (and partner with Rick Tramanto) of Tru in Chicago, host of the Food Network's *Sweet Dreams*, and a James Beard Award Winner.

Combining the concept of her acclaimed Four-Course Dessert Collection with childhood memories of the Kellogg's Variety pack, she has created the ultimate Cereal Sampler: one plate, with three different bite-size sweets—each using a different favorite brand.

FRESH RASPBERRY CARAMELIZED RICE PUDDING

PUDDING

½ cup arborio rice, rinsed
2 cups whole milk
¼ vanilla bean, split
6 tablespoons sugar

In a strainer, rinse the rice under cold water to remove some of the starch. In a medium saucepan, simmer the rice with the milk and vanilla bean until very tender, about 20 to 25 minutes. When it's done, stir in the sugar.

They snap with energy, crackle with fun, pop up the muscles for everyone!

TOPPING

¾ cup sugar
6 tablespoons water
2 cups Rice Krispies
1 tablespoon butter

1. Pour the sugar into the center of a saucepan fitted with a candy thermometer. Carefully pour the water around the walls of the pan, trying not to splash any sugar onto the walls. Do not stir; gently draw your finger twice through the center of the sugar, making a cross, to moisten it.

2. Over high heat, bring the mixture to a full boil and cook without stirring until the mixture reaches the soft-ball stage (240 degrees), about 5 to 10 minutes. Turn off the heat and stir in the cereal. Turn the heat back on high and continue cooking while stirring until caramelized and golden in color. Turn off the heat and stir in the butter to help stop the cooking.

3. Pour onto a silicone baking mat (such as a Silpat) on the counter or a marble surface and let it cool about 5 minutes; then break it up. Store in an airtight container for up to 1 week.

TO ASSEMBLE

1 pint fresh raspberries

Pick through the berries and place half of them (divided equally) in the bottom of egg cups, espresso cups, or cordial glasses. Spoon the cooked rice pudding over the berries, then top the pudding with the remaining berries. Sprinkle with the caramelized rice cereal. If desired, chill the cooked rice over an ice bath to make it ahead of time and serve the dish cold.

☞ Makes 8-10 servings

Kellogg's

RICE
KRISPIES

PACKING

MAR 8 1963

STARTED

"The Best to You Each Morning"

Pop!

FREE
"Milk Money"

MILK

(See Package Back)

REGULAR

NET WT. 5-1/2 OZ.

PEANUT BUTTER-KRISPY COCOA CHEWIES

4 cups Cocoa Krispies
3/4 cup dried cherries
1/2 cup light brown sugar
1/2 cup light corn syrup
1/2 cup creamy or crunchy peanut butter

Tastes like a chocolate milkshake— only crunchy.

1. In a large bowl, combine the cereal and cherries.

2. In a small saucepan, combine the brown sugar and corn syrup and bring to a boil. Boil for 1 minute, then turn off the heat. Stir in the peanut butter.

3. Pour it over the cereal and cherries, stirring immediately to combine and coat. Press into a buttered 8 × 8-inch pan and let cool to set (about 15 minutes). Store at room temperature. When ready to serve, cut into 2-inch squares, then cut the squares on the diagonal into triangles. Allot 2 triangles per serving, leaning one on the other.

Makes about 32 chewies

Kellogg's

COCOA KRISPIES

Chocolate
lavored Rice

NET WT. 9 OZ.

Coco-lossal Summertime Treat
**CRUNCHY
ICE CREAM BARS**

(SEE PACKAGE BACK)

GOLDEN FROOT CUPCAKES

¼ cup (4 tablespoons) unsalted butter
½ cup sugar
¼ teaspoon vanilla
1 egg
¾ cup sifted all-purpose flour
¾ teaspoon baking powder
⅛ teaspoon salt
¼ cup whole milk
¾ cup Froot Loops
Powdered sugar

*Follow my nose,
it always knows.*

1. Using a mixer with a whip attachment, cream the butter until light and fluffy. Add the sugar and continue to cream. Gradually, add the vanilla and egg, mixing in well.

2. In a medium bowl, sift together the flour, baking powder, and salt. Mix into the butter mixture alternating with the milk in 3 batches.

3. Preheat the oven to 350 degrees.

4. Pour the batter into mini muffin pans lined with cupcake paper liners, filling them ¾ full, and sprinkle the tops with a generous pinch (6 pieces) of Froot Loops. Bake for 8 to 10 minutes, until the cupcakes are puffed and firm in the center and light golden brown on the edges. Serve with a light dusting of powdered sugar.

☞ **Makes 18 mini cupcakes**

ROASTED GARLIC-LEMON ARTICHOKES

1 whole lemon

2 large artichokes with stems

6 cups Cheerios

1/2 cup olive oil

1/2 cup white wine

1/4 cup chopped fresh mint

3 anchovy fillets, minced

5 to 6 cloves garlic, minced

1 tablespoon grated lemon peel

Freshly ground black pepper, to taste

2 lemon slices

2 garlic cloves, halved

Salt to taste

1. Preheat the oven to 375 degrees.

2. Fill a large bowl with water. Squeeze the juice from the whole lemon into the water. Cut off all but 1/2 inches of stems from the artichokes. Peel the stems with a vegetable peeler. Starting at the bottom of each artichoke, snap off the outer 3 rows of leaves. Cut off the top half of each artichoke. Spread the leaves, exposing the center. Cut out the center leaves and bristly choke. Place the artichokes in the lemon water. Set aside.

One in every eleven boxes of cereal sold is a Cheerios product.

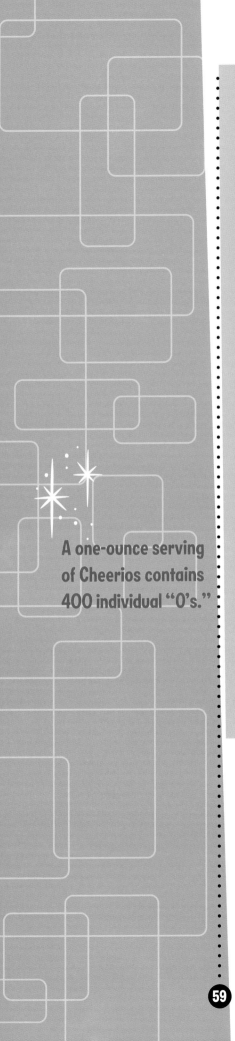

3. In a large bowl, combine the Cheerios with ¼ cup of the olive oil, the mint, anchovies, garlic, and lemon peel. Mix thoroughly. Season to taste with the pepper.

4. Drain the artichokes, then stuff the centers with Cheerios mixture. Top each artichoke with a lemon slice, then invert into 13 × 9-inch baking dish. Add ½ inch water to pan. Add garlic halves. Drizzle artichokes with the remaining ¼ cup of oil and sprinkle with salt and pepper to taste. Cover with foil and roast 1¼ hours, or until artichokes are very tender.

5. Transfer the artichokes to a platter and serve warm or at room temperature.

 Serves 4

A one-ounce serving of Cheerios contains 400 individual "O's."

THE *Goodness* OF TOASTED OATS

General *G* Mills

Cheerios

STUFFED PORK TENDERLOIN

If you know your oats, you, too, will go . . . For the power breakfast, Cheerios!

Before **PILAR SANCHEZ** (with her husband, Didier Lenders) opened Pilar in Napa in 2004, she had worked as a sous chef, chef, Chef de Cuisine, and Executive Chef in high-profile dining rooms from Santa Barbara to San Francisco to St. Helena, had run her own restaurant in Paris, and had co-hosted the Food Network's *Melting Pot's Mediterranean Table*. Yet although Sanchez has spent two decades surrounded by some of the best food in the world, she concedes that when she finally makes it home in the evening and goes to fix something to eat, her nightly meal of choice is a bowl of cereal.

1 pork tenderloin (2 to 2 1/2 pounds)
1/2 cup (8 tablespoons) unsalted butter
1 small yellow onion, finely diced
2 stalks celery, finely diced
1/2 cup dried apricots, finely diced
1/3 cup pitted prunes, finely diced
1 teaspoon chopped fresh sage
1 teaspoon chopped fresh thyme
Salt and black pepper to taste
2 cups Honey Nut Cheerios
1/4 cup toasted pecans, roughly chopped
2 large Yukon gold potatoes
1 large sweet potato
1 tablespoon honey
3/4 cup chicken stock
2 tablespoons chopped fresh parsley

1. To prepare the tenderloin for stuffing, first make sure it is relatively free of fat. The side muscle should be removed as well as any silver skin. Butterfly the entire tenderloin by running a boning knife lengthwise down the center, cutting through only half the muscle. Spread the tenderloin out with your hands and then cut the entire length of each side, again only halfway. The three cuts should have now spread out the tenderloin. Take a piece of plastic wrap and lay it over the meat. Using the flat side of a small skillet, gently pound the tenderloin to create a flat surface. Place the meat back in the refrigerator while you prepare the stuffing.

2. In a large skillet over low heat, melt ¼ cup (4 tablespoons) of the butter. Start by cooking the onion alone (still over low heat) until it is translucent and aromatic. Add the celery, apricots, and prunes. Turn the heat up to medium, and stir while continuing to cook another 3 minutes. Turn off heat, and add the fresh sage and thyme. (It's always best to chop these just before throwing them into the pan.) Stir well, then season with salt and pepper. Let the mixture cool to room temperature.

3. Using a large knife, chop the Honey Nut Cheerios very roughly. Do not use a food processor or they will be pulverized. Add the Honey Nut Cheerios and pecans to the cooled fruit-vegetable mixture, stirring well to incorporate. Adjust the seasoning.

4. Preheat the oven to 450 degrees.

5. Lay the butterflied pork tenderloin out onto a clean cutting board and sprinkle with salt and pepper. Spoon the stuffing down atop the meat, and spread it out into an even layer. Roll the meat over itself, creating a pinwheel, and leaving the seam side down on the cutting board. When done, roll the small tip of the tenderloin under. Using at least 10 pieces of butcher twine cut into 8-inch lengths, tie the tenderloin at about 1½-inch intervals. Tie securely, but not so tight as to squish out the stuffing.

6. Sprinkle all sides of the meat with salt and pepper. Place a small square of aluminum foil around each end of the pinwheel, then set the tenderloin in a casserole dish. Put the pork, uncovered, into the hot oven.

7. While it cooks, wash the potatoes and sweet potato well before cutting them into 1-inch chunks. Sprinkle with salt and pepper, then place them into the casserole dish along with the pork tenderloin. Break the remaining 4 tablespoons butter into smaller pieces and place randomly throughout the dish.

8. Turn the oven down to 400 degrees. Continue cooking for 20 minutes, until the internal temperature of the tenderloin reaches 130 degrees (according a meat themometer), and the potatoes are done and tender.

9. After removing the dish from the oven, lift the roast and place atop a cooling rack with a sheet pan underneath to catch the drippings. Using a slotted spoon, stir the cooked potatoes to coat, then remove them from the dish and arrange around a serving platter. Place the casserole dish onto a stove burner and turn to medium heat. Add the honey and bring it to a simmer. Add the chicken stock and turn up the heat. Stir well with a whisk, adjust the seasoning, and turn off the heat.

10. Slice the pork into 2-inch pieces, arranging them on the platter with the potatoes. Carefully pour the sauce over the meat and potatoes, then sprinkle with the freshly chopped parsley.

☞ Serves 4

In 1997, among the workers earning $12 per hour sweeping up Cheerios dust from the floor of the General Mills factory in Cedar Rapids, Iowa, was a biochemical engineering student named Ashton Kutcher.

SHREDDED SHRIMP WITH PINEAPPLE-MANGO SALSA

In 1892, **HENRY PERKY**, a lawyer living in Watertown, New York, built a contraption that would press boiled wheat into filaments, which could then be shaped and baked into easily digestible biscuits. Hoping to sell his patented "cereal machine" to others who also suffered from stomach troubles, he rode around in a horse-drawn carriage, passing out free samples of the dried wheat snack his invention could make. However, when it quickly became clear that it was the pillow-shaped biscuits—and not the appliance—that people wanted to buy, Perky dropped plans to market the machine, relocated to Boston, and opened a bakery operation called the Shredded Wheat Company. Other locations followed, and in 1928, Perky, who had moved to Niagara Falls, sold his business to Nabisco.

SALSA

1 cup diced fresh pineapple
1/2 cup chopped mango chutney
1/2 cup minced red onion
1/3 cup chopped fresh cilantro
1 jalapeño pepper, stemmed, seeded, and minced
2 tablespoons lime juice

In a small bowl, combine the pineapple, chutney, red onion, cilantro, jalapeño, and lime juice. Set aside.

SHRIMP

1/3 cup cornstarch
1/2 teaspoon salt
1/2 teaspoon cayenne pepper
3 egg whites
3 large-size Shredded Wheat biscuits, crumbled into shreds
24 large shrimp with tails, peeled, deveined, and butterflied
Vegetable oil for deep frying

1. In a medium bowl, combine the cornstarch, salt, and cayenne.

2. In another medium bowl, beat the egg whites until frothy.

3. Place the crushed cereal in a pie plate.

4. Flatten the shrimp, then dip in the cornstarch mixture, shaking off the excess. Next, dip in the egg whites, then press into the cereal mixture. Turn the shrimp and press into the cereal mixture again to coat both sides. Arrange on a baking sheet or tray.

5. Pour enough oil into a heavy pot to reach a depth of 2 inches. Heat to 350 degrees.

6. Working in batches, add the shrimp to the hot oil and fry until cooked through, about 1 minute. Remove with slotted spoon and drain on paper towels.

7. Arrange the shrimp on a platter around the salsa for dipping.

☞ **Serves 12 as appetizer, 6 as main course**

CURRIED PILAF

2 tablespoons olive oil

1 medium onion, chopped

2 teaspoons curry powder

1 cup brown basmati rice

1/2 teaspoon salt

2 cups chicken or vegetable stock

1/3 cup finely chopped dried apricots

2 tablespoons butter

1 large Shredded Wheat biscuit, crumbled into shreds

1/3 cup coarsely chopped walnuts, toasted

1. In a medium saucepan, heat the oil over medium heat. Add the onion and sauté until softened. Stir in the curry powder and cook 30 seconds. Add the rice and cook, stirring, 1 minute. Stir in the salt and stock and bring to a boil. Reduce the heat to low, cover, and cook 20 minutes.

2. Remove the pan from the heat. Add the apricots, fluffing the rice with a fork, and let stand, covered, 5 minutes.

3. Meanwhile, in a small skillet, melt the butter over medium heat. Add the cereal shreds and sauté until browned, about 1 minute. Add to the rice along with the walnuts. Toss and serve.

 Serves 4

CEREAL KILLER

(Corn Poppler with Roasted Peaches, Corn Pops Nougat, Vanilla Anglaise, and Blueberry Sorbet)

Owner of the New York–based restaurant and consulting firm Seven-One-Ate, **JAMES DISTEFANO** made his mark as a pastry chef (and later executive pastry chef) at a string of Manhattan's hippest joints, including the Park Avenue Cafe, Bluefin, and davidburke&donatella. Twice recognized by *New York* magazine as the hands behind some of the city's best desserts (including a stellar butterscotch panna cotta), and always one step ahead of the sugar curve, he was actually using cereal in his recipes even before we asked. While this dish involves multiple steps and elements, it is designed so that all the components can be made at least a day in advance, then assembled quickly before serving.

CORN POPPLER

½ cup plus 1 tablespoon (9 tablespoons total) unsalted butter
1 teaspoon kosher salt
1 teaspoon vanilla extract
24 ounces mini marshmallows
10 cups Corn Pops

1. In a medium sauté pan melt the butter with the salt and vanilla extract over a medium-low heat.

2. Stir in the marshmallows. Mix with a wooden spoon, keeping the heat mediun-low. This will help avoid scorching the mixture.

3. Once the marshmallows have melted, add the Corn Pops and stir to coat evenly.

4. Spread the mixture onto a small baker's tray lined with wax paper.

5. To ensure that the treat has been spread evenly, place another piece of wax paper over the top of the Corn Pops and gently press down using another baker's tray of the same size. Once the confection has cooled to room temperature, wrap with plastic wrap and place in the refrigerator for 2 hours.

6. To serve, cut the Corn Poppler into 2-inch squares.

ROASTED PEACHES

4 ripe peaches
2 cups sugar
1 tablespoon vanilla extract

1. Preheat the oven to 300 degrees.

2. Cut the peaches in half following the circumference of the peach. Use the stone as your guide. To separate the two halves, gently twist in opposite directions. Remove the stone from one half of the peach and discard. In a bowl, toss the peach halves with the sugar and the vanilla.

3. Sprinkle some of the vanilla sugar onto a baking sheet and place the peaches (cut side down) onto the sugar.

4. Place the peaches in the preheated oven and bake until tender. This will take about 12 to 18 minutes. To check, use a toothpick to pierce the skin of the peach. The peach should offer hardly any resistance. Once the peaches are done, remove them from the oven and cover the baking tray with plastic wrap (for 10 to 15 minutes, maximum; do not allow the peaches to get cold). The steam that the peaches emit will allow you to peel the skins easier.

5. Peel the peaches and place them in an airtight container. Keep refrigerated.

So as not to alienate nutrition-minded parents, a number of classic brands excised the word sugar from their names in the early 1990s.

Kellogg's
SUGAR
POPS

POPPIN' GOOD

NET WT. 9 OZ.

Kellogg's SUGAR POPS

SUGAR POPS
PETE

BOYS! GIRLS!

MAN-MADE FISH THAT REALLY SWIM!

"MAGIC Aquarium"

(See Package Back)

REGULAR SIZE
NET WT. 8 OZ.

Sugar Pops are tops!

VANILLA ANGLAISE

4 ounces sugar ($1/3$ cup plus 2 tablespoons)
2 tablespoons vanilla extract
1 pint half and half
6 egg yolks

1. In a stainless-steel pot over medium heat, combine the sugar and vanilla with $1\frac{1}{2}$ cups of the half and half. Cook until the mixture boils.

2. Mix the egg yolks with the remaining $1/2$ cup of the half and half, then whisk in one-third of the heated cream mixture.

3. Pour the egg yolk mixture back into the cream mixture, stirring with a wooden spoon over low heat until the sauce thickens to coat the back of a spoon. Do not bring this mixture to a boil or the egg yolks will curdle. The mix will only thicken slightly.

4. Strain through a fine sieve into a container large enough to hold the sauce. Set the container into a large bowl of ice water to cool, stirring occasionally. Store in an airtight container in the refrigerator.

CORN POPS NOUGAT

$1/4$ cup (4 tablespoons) unsalted butter
1 cup sugar
$1/4$ teaspoon kosher salt
1 cup Corn Pops

1. In a medium sauté pan over medium heat, combine the butter, sugar, and salt. Melt the butter and caramelize the sugar. Stir the mixture frequently.

2. Once the caramel reaches an amber color (about 7 to 10 minutes), stir in the Corn Pops.

3. Mix to evenly coat. Pour the mixture onto a wax paper-lined baker's tray and spread out into a thin layer. Let it cool at room temperature. Break apart the nougat and store in an airtight container at room temperature.

BLUEBERRY SORBET

2 cups water

7/8 cup sugar

1 tablespoon freshly squeezed lemon juice

1 cup fresh blueberries, pureed and strained

1. Place the water, sugar, and lemon juice in a small pot and bring to a boil over medium-high heat. Once the syrup has boiled, remove it from the heat and chill it completely over a bowl of ice water.

2. Combine the fresh blueberry puree and the syrup. Mix well.

3. Place the blueberry sorbet base in an ice cream machine and freeze according to the manufacturer's instructions. Store in an airtight container in the freezer.

GARNISH

2 cups fresh blueberries

8 fresh mint sprigs

The pops are sweeter and the taste is new. They're shot with sugar through and through.

TO ASSEMBLE:

1. In the center of a 10-inch plate, place one Corn Poppler square.

2. Slice one roasted peach half into 8 even wedges. Shingle them on top of the square, making sure that it is covered completely with the peaches.

3. Spoon 3 tablespoons of Vanilla Anglaise, then ¼ cup of fresh blueberries around the sides of the square.

4. Place 5 small nuggets of Corn Pop Nougat around the plate as well.

5. Garnish the top of the roasted peaches with a small scoop of Blueberry Sorbet and a sprig of fresh mint.

 Serves 8

TOMATO GRATIN
WITH GRAPE NUTS TOPPING

Cookbook author **MARTHA ROSE SHULMAN**, whose twenty-plus books include *Mediterranean Light, Provençal Light,* and *Ready When You Are,* based this recipe on one of her favorite dishes. "I thought it would work because the tomatoes become very sweet and soft as they bake, and the slight sweetness and crunch of the Grape Nuts is a nice complement."

That's an understatement, as you'll see when you try it with a cold roasted chicken, poached salmon, or just a heel of fresh-baked bread.

2 pounds ripe but firm tomatoes, sliced

Salt to taste

1 teaspoon sugar

¼ cup Grape Nuts

¼ cup fresh bread crumbs

2 tablespoons chopped fresh parsley

2 tablespoons extra-virgin olive oil

1. Preheat the oven to 400 degrees. Oil a 2-quart baking dish.

2. Layer the tomatoes in the dish, sprinkling each layer evenly with salt and sugar.

Grape Nuts are neither grape nor nut; rather, they are made from wheat and barley. The inventor, C. W. Post, came up with the name because the cereal contained maltose (which he incorrectly thought was grape sugar) and because the distinctive flavor reminded him of nuts.

"ALL POST CEREALS HAPPEN TO BE JUST A LITTLE BIT BETTER"

3. Grind the Grape Nuts in a food processor fitted with a steel blade until they have the texture of coarse bread crumbs. Add the bread crumbs, parsley, and olive oil to the processor and blend together. Spread over the top of the tomatoes in an even layer.

4. Bake for 1 hour and turn the heat down to 325 degrees. Bake another 30 minutes to 1 hour, until the top is golden brown and the juices that are left in the pan are thick. Serve warm, at room temperature, or cold.

☞ Serves 4

Before Euell Gibbons ("Ever eat a pine tree?"), before it was touted as the cereal that "fills you up, not out," Post advertised Grape Nuts as an aid for achieving and maintaining sobriety.

During his trip to Antarctica in 1928, Admiral Byrd sustained himself by eating Grape Nuts.

MOCHA-COCOA TOWERS

Makes breakfast taste like chocolate

Many a French patisserie has done a chocolate-espresso recipe similar to this one, though they're apt to use Gaufrettes (an expensive wafer cookie) in the crust. Cocoa Puffs, at three or four dollars a box (versus eighteen dollars a tin) aren't only cheaper, but (just between us) they actually work better.

¼ cup (4 tablespoons) butter

1½ cups chopped high-quality milk chocolate

6 cups Cocoa Puffs

½ cup chopped toasted almonds

1½ cups chopped 55 percent semisweet chocolate

1 tablespoon instant espresso powder

1 cup heavy cream

2 tablespoons cocoa powder

1. Line a 9-inch square pan with plastic wrap or waxed paper, allowing the excess to extend over the pan edges.

2. In a small pan, melt the butter. Add the milk chocolate and stir over low heat until the chocolate is completely melted.

General Mills

cocoa puffs

★ TV ★
PLAYING CARDS

SET #1

and
2 CARD GAMES
(SEE PACKAGE BACK)

Goodness IN CHOCOLATE
FLAVOR CORN PUFFS

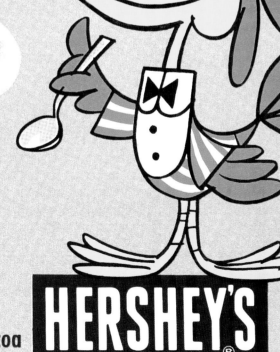

K

 Made with HERSHEY'S cocoa

HERSHEY'S ®

NET WT. 9 OZ.

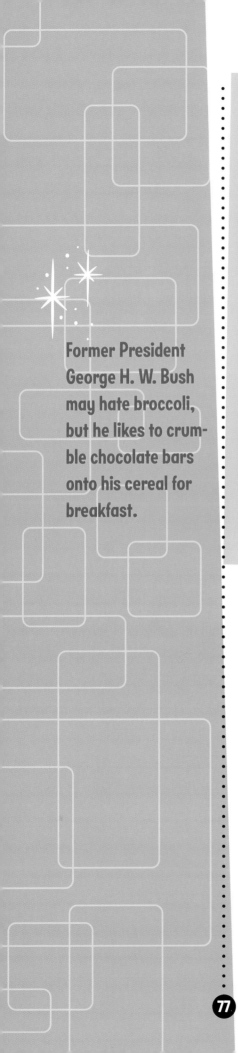

3. In a food processor, combine the Cocoa Puffs and almonds. Process until coarsely ground. Add the melted chocolate mixture and process just until blended.

4. Transfer the mixture to a prepared pan and press onto the bottom in an even layer. Chill 1 hour, until firm.

5. In top of a double boiler set over hot, not boiling water, melt the semi-sweet chocolate. Cool slightly.

6. Dissolve the espresso powder in 2 tablespoons hot water. Cool.

7. Whip the cream with the espresso and powdered sugar until it holds soft peaks. Fold into the cooled semisweet chocolate. Spread this mixture over the chocolate crust. Chill until set.

8. Using the edges of plastic wrap or waxed paper, carefully lift the dessert from the pan. Dust with cocoa powder. Cut into thirds, then from the short side, cut each third into 8 slices about 1 inch wide.

☞ **Makes 24 servings**

It has to be good because they named it after me!

CAP'N CRUNCH CRAB CAKES

From the day Planet Hollywood opened, Crunch Chicken has been the number one seller for the restaurant chain—and, for many, about the only thing worth ordering on the menu. This version takes the venerable Captain to a new level—sea level—where the sweetness of the cereal is the perfect contrast to the spiciness of the cake.

3/4 cup mayonnaise
1 tablespoon Thai chili-garlic sauce
1 tablespoon lime juice
1/2 teaspoon grated lime peel
1 pound lump crab meat
1/2 cup chopped fresh cilantro
1/3 cup chopped red onion
1 egg, lightly beaten
3 cups panko flakes (Japanese-style bread crumbs)
2 cups crushed Cap'n Crunch (about 3 1/2 cups uncrushed)
Vegetable oil for frying

1. In a small bowl, blend the mayonnaise, chili-garlic sauce, lime juice, and lime peel.

2. In a large bowl, combine the crab meat, cilantro, and onion. Stir in 1/3 cup of the mayonnaise mixture and the egg. Reserve the remaining mayonnaise mixture for garnish.

3. In a third bowl, combine the panko flakes and Cap'n Crunch. Stir 1 1/2 cups into the crab mixture. Form into 1/2-inch-thick cakes, using 1/2 cup mixture for each.

4. Dredge the cakes in the remaining Cap'n Crunch mixture. Arrange in a single layer on a tray or baking sheet. Chill at least 1 hour or up to 8 hours.

5. In a large skillet, heat 2 tablespoons oil over medium-high heat. Working in batches, add the crab cakes and cook until golden brown and cooked through, about 4 minutes per side, adding more oil as needed.

6. Serve hot, topped with a dollop of the remaining mayonnaise mixture.

 **Makes 8 crab cakes**

It's got corn for crunch, oats for punch, and it stays crunchy even in milk.

In 1963, eyeing the success of Jay Ward's *Rocky and Bullwinkle*, Quaker Oats turned to the animator and asked him to create a character they could use to sell a breakfast cereal. Their only directive: Market research had told them that the number-one thing kids wanted in a cereal was that it didn't get soggy when wet. Ward came back with a (sea) captain named Crunch (full name: Horatio Magellan Crunch), his ship (the S.S. *Guppy*), and a crew of four kids (and a dog). Quaker sparked to the concept, commissioning Ward's studio to film a series of commercials for TV. However, it wasn't until after seeing and approving the finished spots that Quaker actually got around to formulating (and manufacturing) a real cereal to go with the already existing ads.

STAFF OF LIFE POTATO PANCAKES

The Life cereal ad featuring Mikey ("Let Mikey try it. He hates everything.") aired nationally from 1972 through 1984, making it the single longest-running commercial in television history.

CRÈME FRAÎCHE

1 cup heavy cream
2 tablespoons buttermilk

Combine the heavy cream and buttermilk in a glass container. Cover and let stand at room temperature 8 to 24 hours or until thick. Stir well, then cover and refrigerate up to 10 days.

PANCAKES

2 large baking potatoes, peeled and finely shredded (about 4 cups)
2 tablespoons chopped fresh chives
2 eggs, lightly beaten
1/2 cup crushed Life cereal (about 3/4 cup uncrushed)
Salt and freshly ground black pepper
Vegetable oil for frying
6 ounces smoked salmon, cut into 12 thin slices
3 tablespoons caviar

1. In a large bowl, combine the potatoes, chives, and eggs. Stir in cereal, and season to taste with the salt and pepper.

2. Preheat oven to 200 degrees.

3. Pour the oil into a large skillet to depth of 1/8 inch. Heat over medium-high. Using 2 spoons, drop the mixture by large spoonfuls into the hot oil, flattening with the back of the spoon to form 3-inch circles. Fry until deep golden brown and crisp on one side, about 5 minutes, then turn, and cook the second side until deep golden and crisp. Drain the pancakes on paper towels, then transfer to a baking sheet and keep warm in oven.

4. Top each pancake with a spoonful of crème fraîche, a slice of smoked salmon, and a scant teaspoon of caviar.

 **Makes about 12 pancakes**

life

QUAKER ®

The Delicious High Protein Cereal

TRY THE CEREAL MIKEY LIKES!

10¢ Coupon inside

Net Wt 15 oz · 425g

ROASTED POBLANO MEAT LOAF

By 1950, sales of their forty-something-year-old Ralston Wheat Cereal were sagging, so Ralston Purina decided it could broaden the brand's appeal by making it more kid-friendly. Company executives left the formula intact; instead, inspired by the recognition factor of their highly popular checkerboard logo, they simply changed the name—to Chex.

2 poblano chiles

2 pounds ground beef

1 small onion, minced

1/2 cup shredded manchego cheese (Monterey Jack can be substituted)

1 cup chopped fresh cilantro

1 teaspoon ground cumin

2 eggs, lightly beaten

2 cups crushed Corn Chex (about 3 1/2 cups uncrushed)

Salt and black pepper

Salsa, guacamole, and sour cream

1. Roast the chiles under the broiler, turning often until blackened all over. Enclose in paper bag for 10 minutes.

2. Preheat the oven to 350 degrees. Oil a 9 × 5 inch loaf pan.

3. Wearing latex gloves, rub the charred skin from the chiles. Stem the chiles, then cut into halves and remove the seeds. Dice the chiles finely and place in a large bowl. Add the ground beef, onion, cheese, cilantro, cumin, and eggs. Add the cereal and mix thoroughly. Season to taste with salt and pepper.

4. Pat the mixture into the prepared loaf pan. Bake until an instant-read meat thermometer inserted into the center reads 160 degrees, about 1 hour. Let stand 10 minutes.

5. Remove the meat loaf from the pan and slice. Serve topped with your favorite salsa, guacamole, or sour cream.

 Serves 6 to 8

FLAVOR
MINERALS
PROTEINS
VITAMINS
ENERGY

BITE SIZE Wheat Chex

BITE SIZE Rice Chex

They had their BITE SIZE CHEX today!

(How about you?)

THERE IS A DIFFERENCE IN CEREALS

No other cereal, flaked or puffed, gives you so much honest-to-goodness nourishment in such concentrated Bite Size form. Delicious? Yes. Crisp? Down to the last bite. But best of all is the wonderful ready-for-anything feeling you have after a Bite Size Chex breakfast. Don't miss it. Start tomorrow.

WHEAT CHEX

RICE CHEX

SO NOURISHING! Every crisp bite whole-grain-rich in vitamin B₁, niacin, and iron.

RALSTON PURINA COMPANY, St. Louis, Mo

CORN
CHEX ®

BITE-SIZE TOASTED CORN

®

Here's a fresh, nutty idea for your next party

CHEX PARTY MIX®

It's so easy to fix, why wait for a party.

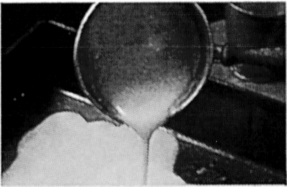

1 Heat oven to 250°. Slowly melt 6 TABLE-SPOONS BUTTER OR MARGARINE in a shallow pan.

2 Stir in 4 TEASPOONS WORCESTERSHIRE SAUCE AND 1 TEASPOON SEASONED SALT (or ¼ teaspoon garlic powder and ¼ teaspoon salt.)

3 Add 8 CUPS CHEX (Mix Wheat, Corn, and Rice equally or anyway you like)

4 Add ¾ CUP SALTED NUTS. Mix until all pieces are coated. Heat in oven 45 minutes. Stir every 15 minutes. Spread on absorbent paper to cool. Yield: 8¾ cups.

4-737-266 of Related Company   Printed in U.S.A.

CHEX-ITS

1½ cups Wheat Chex
1 cup all-purpose flour
2 teaspoons baking powder
1 teaspoon sugar
½ teaspoon baking soda
¼ teaspoon salt
⅓ cup butter, chilled and cut into small pieces
½ cup buttermilk

1. Preheat the oven to 350 degrees.

2. Place the cereal in a food processor and pulse until finely ground.

3. Add the flour, baking powder, sugar, baking soda, and salt and process to blend.

4. Add the cold butter pieces and pulse until the mixture looks crumbly.

5. With the machine running, pour in the buttermilk and continue to process until a dough forms.

6. Turn out onto a well-floured board and knead 10 times. Roll the dough into the rectangle slightly larger than 15 × 10 inches. Trim the edges, then cut into 2 × 1½-inch crackers.

7. Transfer the crackers to a baking sheet and bake 15 minutes or until deep golden and crisp. Cool on wire rack. Store in an airtight container. Serve with **NUTTY APPLE BLUE CHEESE TERRINE** as well as any spread, tapanade, or dip.

 **Makes 50 crackers**

NUTTY APPLE
BLUE CHEESE TERRINE

½ cup chopped walnuts

½ cup lightly crushed Apple Jacks (about ¾ cup uncrushed)

2 tablespoons light corn syrup

½ teaspoon salt

Cayenne pepper, to taste

8 ounces cream cheese, at room temperature

⅓ cup crumbled blue cheese

1. Preheat the oven to 325 degrees.

2. In a small bowl, combine the walnuts, Apple Jacks, corn syrup, salt, and cayenne pepper.

A is for Apple,
J is for Jacks
Cinnamon toasty
Apple Jacks!

3. Spread evenly on a lightly oiled baking sheet and bake 15 minutes, stirring several times. Cool completely. Break up any clumps.

4. In a small bowl, combine the cream cheese and blue cheese. Beat to blend thoroughly.

5. Line a 2-cup mold or bowl with plastic wrap. Place the cheese mixture in a bowl and smooth the surface with a spatula. Cover and chill at least 1 hour.

6. To serve, invert the cheese onto a serving plate and remove the plastic wrap. Press the cereal mixture onto the surface of the cheese. Serve with **CHEX-ITS**.

Serves 6 to 8

A bowl a day keeps the bullies away.

Kellogg's
APPLE JACKS

APPLE-CINNAMON COATED CEREAL

KIDS! Go sky-spotting with a
"DICK DASTARDLY"
AiRPLANE·TeLeSCoPe
(See package back)

WT 7 OZ

ORANGE-GINGER WHITE CHOCOLATE BISCOTTI

Each piece of Honeycomb has exactly seven holes, to resemble a bee-made honeycomb, which consists of seven hexagonal wax cells.

4 cups crushed Honeycomb (about 6 cups uncrushed)
1 1/2 cups buttermilk baking mix
1/2 cup chopped almonds
1/2 cup chopped candied ginger
Grated peel of 1 small orange
1/4 teaspoon ground ginger
4 eggs, lightly beaten
1 cup chopped white chocolate

1. Preheat the oven to 350 degrees.

2. In a large bowl, combine the crushed Honeycomb, baking mix, almonds, candied ginger, orange peel, and ground ginger. Blend well.

3. Add the eggs and blend well. The dough will be crumbly. Gather the dough into 2 equal portions.

4. On a floured surface, shape each portion into a log about 10 inches long. Place about 3 inches apart on the baking sheet and bake 40 minutes, or until firm and golden brown. Cool on a wire rack.

5. Reduce the oven heat to 300 degrees.

6. With a long serrated knife, cut the logs on the extreme diagonal into 1/2-inch-thick slices.

7. Place the slices, cut sides down, on the baking sheet and bake 20 minutes. Turn and bake 20 minutes longer. Cool on wire rack.

8. Place the white chocolate in the top of a double boiler. Set over simmering water until the chocolate is completely melted. Stir until smooth. Dip one cut side of each biscotti into the chocolate, then transfer to wire rack to cool with chocolate side up. (If necessary, the biscotti can be placed in the refrigerator to set the chocolate.)

9. Store in an airtight container.

☞ **Makes about 18 biscotti**

HAZELNUT CHICKEN WITH MUSTARD SAUCE

ART SMITH is the James Beard Award–winning author of *Back to the Table* and *Kitchen Life*, and the personal chef to Oprah Winfrey. His nutty baked chicken hits a home run, turning the "breakfast of champions" into a winning dinner entrée.

CHICKEN

1 cup raw hazelnuts
1 cup Wheaties, crushed (about 2 cups uncrushed)
3 tablespoons Dijon mustard
1 tablespoon chopped fresh rosemary
1 egg white
4 chicken breasts, boneless and skinless (about 4 to 6 ounces each)
Salt and black pepper to taste
2 tablespoons vegetable oil

1. Preheat the oven to 400 degrees.

2. Using a food processor, grind the hazelnuts to coarse, then place in a bowl and add the crushed Wheaties.

3. In another bowl, combine the mustard, rosemary, and egg white, and beat well. Flatten the chicken until even and season with the salt and pepper. Lay the breasts in the egg mixture, coating completely, and chill for at least 30 minutes.

4. Once chilled, remove the chicken from the refrigerator and dredge through the hazelnut-cereal combination.

5. Pour the oil into a sauté pan over medium heat. Quickly brown the chicken for 1 to 2 minutes on both sides, being careful not to burn the crust. To finish cooking, remove the breasts from the pan, lay them on a nonstick baking sheet that has been sprayed with cooking spray, and place the tray in the preheated oven for an additional 10 to 12 minutes, or until cooked through.

MUSTARD SAUCE

· · · · · · · · · · ·

2 tablespoons minced shallots

½ cup white wine

¼ cup white wine vinegar

1 tablespoon all-purpose flour

1 tablespoon heavy cream

½ cup (8 tablespoons) unsalted butter, softened

2 tablespoons Dijon mustard

In a saucepan over medium heat, combine the shallots, white wine, and white wine vinegar. Reduce the liquid until almost evaporated, then reduce the heat. Dissolve the flour with a portion of the cream and add it to the pan. Stir in the rest of the cream and reduce. Mix in the softened butter one tablespoon at a time, followed by the mustard. Blend well, pour over the chicken, and serve.

☞ **Serves 4**

A health clinician in Minneapolis was mixing a batch of bran gruel for his patients when some of the mix accidentally spilled on the hot stove, crackling and sizzling into a crisp flake. He tasted the result, and realizing that the accident had promise, took his discovery to the Washburn Crosby Company—who, in 1921, developed it for market and called the product

WHEATIES.

CARAMELIZED ONION TART

The first athlete to appear on a Wheaties box was baseball great Lou Gehrig in 1924. Michael Jordan has been on the box more than any other athlete—eighteen times, including three appearances with the NBA Champion Chicago Bulls.

PASTRY

2 cups Wheaties
1 1/4 cups all-purpose flour
1/2 teaspoon salt
1/2 cup (8 tablespoons) butter, cut in small cubes and chilled
1/4 cup vegetable shortening, chilled
1/4 cup ice water

1. In a food processor or blender, process the cereal 10 seconds. Add the flour and salt, and process just to blend. Add the butter and shortening, and pulse until the mixture resembles coarse meal. With the machine running, pour in the ice water and process just until incorporated. Gather the dough together and shape into disk. Cover in plastic wrap, and chill for approximately 1 hour.

2. Roll the dough out on a floured surface to 12-inch round. Fit into 10-inch tart pan with removable bottom. Pierce the bottom of the dough all over with a fork. Chill 30 minutes.

3. Preheat the oven to 400 degrees.

4. Line the pastry with foil and fill with pie weights. Bake until set and golden, about 15 minutes. Carefully remove foil and weights and bake until golden all over, about 10 minutes.

In 1937, Wheaties, who sponsored local baseball radio broadcasts on ninety-five stations around the country, held a nationwide contest to find their "most popular announcer." The winner was a play-by-play guy from WHO in Des Moines, Iowa, named Ronald Reagan. His prize was an all-expenses-paid trip to California to visit the Chicago Cubs training camp; while there, he was spotted and asked to screen test for Warner Brothers.

FILLING

• • • • •

6 bacon slices, chopped
2 pounds onions, thinly sliced
1 cup heavy cream
4 eggs
1/2 teaspoon nutmeg
Salt and freshly ground black pepper, to taste

1. Preheat the oven to 400 degrees.

2. In a large skillet, cook the bacon over medium heat until crisp, stirring occasionally. With a slotted spoon, transfer the bacon to paper towels to drain. Pour off all but 3 tablespoons of the drippings in the pan. Add the onions to the skillet and cook over medium heat, just until wilted, about 2 minutes. Cover the skillet and continue to cook until the onions are very soft and pale golden, about 30 minutes, lifting lid and stirring frequently. Return the bacon to the skillet and remove from the heat. Cool slightly.

3. In a large bowl, whisk the cream with the eggs and nutmeg. Stir in the onions and season to taste with the salt and pepper.

4. To finish the tart, carefully pour filling into shell, spreading the onions evenly. Bake at 400 degrees until the filling is set and the top is golden, about 25 minutes. Serve warm or at room temperature.

 Serves 10 to 12 as appetizer, 6 as main course

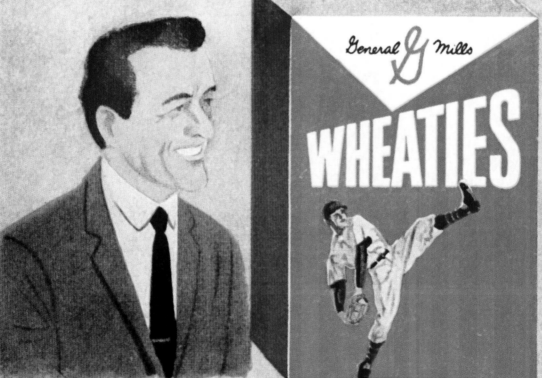

CRISPY RICE AND MILK CHOCOLATE NAPOLEON

SHERRY YARD is a James Beard Award winner, best-selling author of *The Secrets of Baking*, and the reason a staggering 75 percent of the diners at Spago order dessert (and not just for the table to share—we're talking one per guest). As executive pastry chef at one of the most famous restaurants in the world, her food may have been described as "sophisticated," "show stopping," and "spectacular," but none of that has stopped Yard from mixing the exotic with down-home ingredients—including cereal. The following is a version of her popular Napoleon. For best results, she suggests using Erewhon Crispy Brown Rice; however, for the pop culture purist, Rice Krispies could be substituted.

CRISPY RICE WAFERS

2 tablespoons (2 ounces) orange blossom honey
2 tablespoons (2 ounces) glucose
4 cups Erewhon Crispy Brown Rice

1. Preheat the oven to 325 degrees.

2. Place the honey and glucose in a microwave-proof bowl. Microwave on low power 5 to 10 seconds until the mixture is just warmed and has a thin viscosity. Add the rice cereal and stir until evenly incorporated.

3. Spoon out onto a silicone baking mat (such as a Silpat). Place another silicone baking mat on top. With a rolling pin, roll over the top of the silicone baking mat, flattening the rice mixture underneath to a 6 × 6-inch square, ½ inch thick.

4. Bake for 15 to 18 minutes. While still warm, cut into nine 2-inch-square wafers, then remove from the silicone baking mat with an offset spatula and reserve.

MILK CHOCOLATE CREAM

6 ounces milk chocolate, finely chopped
6 ounces heavy cream

1. Place the chopped chocolate in a medium-size mixing bowl.

2. Bring the cream to a boil, then pour over the top of the chopped chocolate.

3. Chill in the refrigerator for 2 hours. Remove and whip until slightly firm, sweetening if desired.

TO ASSEMBLE

2 large bananas, sliced thin

Spoon 2 tablespoons of milk chocolate cream on each plate. Top with a layer of banana slices, then 1 crispy rice wafer. Continue stacking with 2 additional tablespoons of chocolate cream, followed by a second crispy rice wafer. Dust with powdered sugar. Dollop with one last tablespoon of chocolate cream on top. Serve immediately.

 Serves 4

VEGETABLE TEMPURA

TEMPURA COATING

¾ cup all-purpose flour

¾ cup lightly crushed Special K (about 1 cup uncrushed)

2 tablespoons sesame seeds

½ teaspoon salt

One 12-ounce can beer

6 cups assorted sliced vegetables (such as green and red peppers, carrots, zucchini, yams, and onions), as well as whole vegetables (such as sugar snap peas, green beans, or mushrooms), patted dry

Oil for deep frying

1. In a large bowl, combine the flour, cereal, sesame seeds, and salt. Whisk in the beer. Let stand 15 minutes.

2. Heat the oil in a deep fryer to 350 degrees.

3. Working with a few vegetables at a time, dip them in the batter and drop into the hot oil. Fry until golden, about 4 minutes, turning once. Drain on paper towels. Serve hot with dipping sauce and lemon wedges.

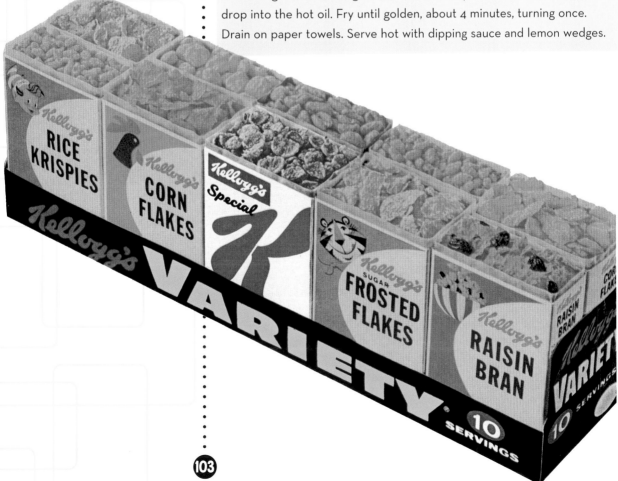

DIPPING SAUCE

· · · · · · · · · ·

2 tablespoons soy sauce

1 tablespoon rice vinegar

2 teaspoons sesame oil

1 teaspoon sugar

A few drops chili oil (optional)

In a small bowl combine the soy sauce, vinegar, sesame oil, and sugar. Stir until the sugar is dissolved. Season to taste with chili oil, if desired.

☞ Serves 4 to 6

"The Special K breakfast keeps my chin up and my weight down."

LEMON YELLOW PIE IN A GLASS

The Trix Rabbit (and his quest for Trix) is the single longest-running ad campaign in television history, having utilized the same character, the same selling line ("Trix is for kids"), and the same plot (the rabbit's foiled attempt to steal a box of cereal) since 1960.

MERINGUE COOKIE CRUST

3 egg whites
1/4 teaspoon salt
1/2 cup sugar
1 1/2 cups finely crushed Trix (yellow and orange pieces only; about 3 cups uncrushed)

1. Preheat the oven to 350 degrees. Line a baking sheet with parchment paper.

2. In the large bowl of an electric mixer, beat the egg whites with salt until foamy. Add 2 tablespoons of the sugar and beat until blended. Continue adding the sugar, 2 tablespoons at a time, until you have used a total of 8 tablespoons (1/2 cup). Continue to beat the mixture until firm peaks form.

3. Fold in the crushed cereal.

4. Drop by tablespoonfuls onto the prepared baking sheet. Bake 15 minutes or until light golden. Leave the meringues in turned-off oven at least 2 hours or until crisp and dry. Remove from the paper and cool on wire rack. Store in an airtight container. These can be made 2 to 3 days in advance.

LEMON MIXTURE

1/4 cup (4 tablespoons) butter
1/3 cup freshly squeezed lemon juice
1 tablespoon grated lemon peel
1/2 cup sugar
3 egg yolks
1 whole egg

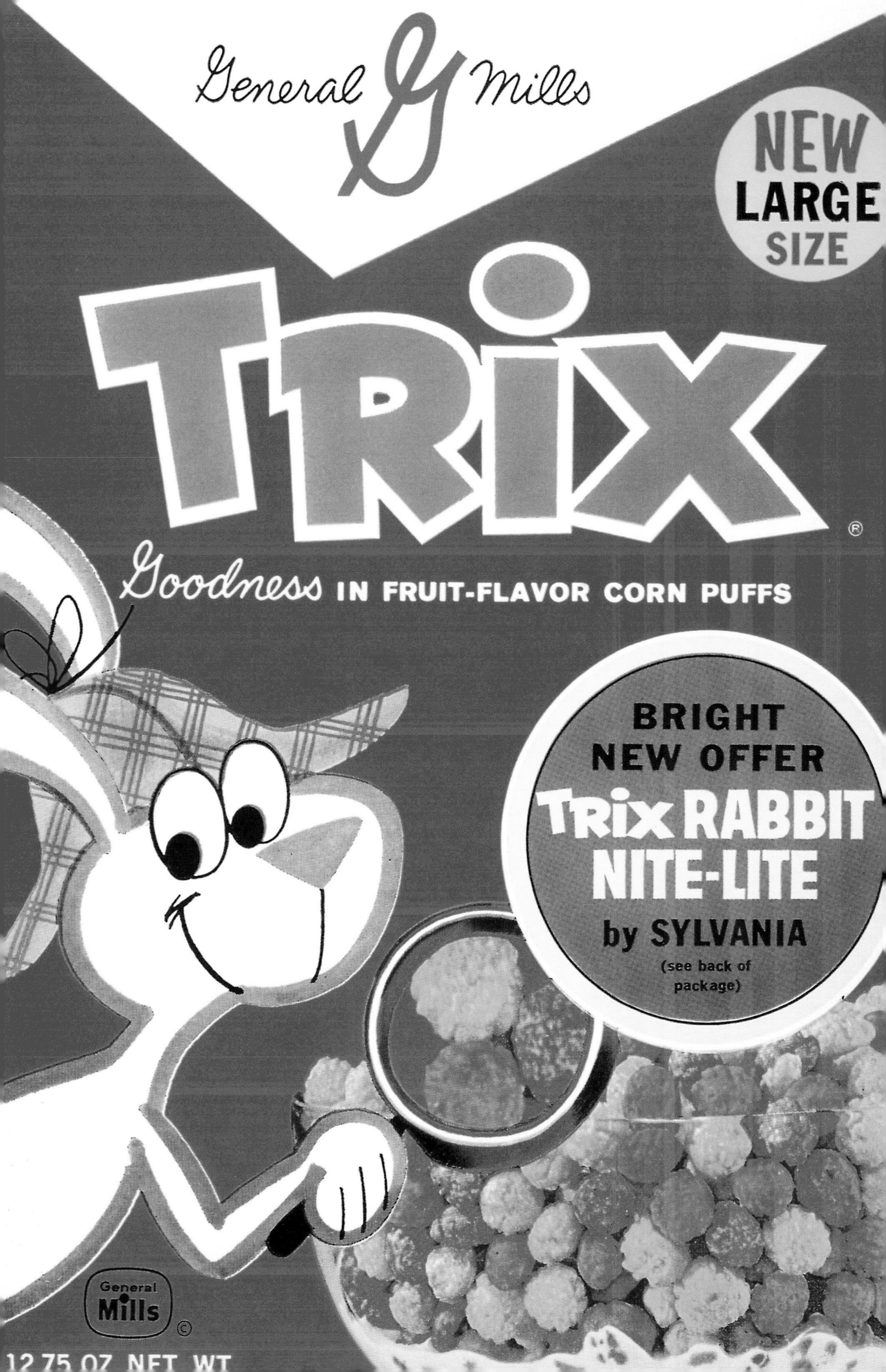
General Mills
NEW LARGE SIZE
TRIX®
Goodness IN FRUIT-FLAVOR CORN PUFFS
BRIGHT NEW OFFER
TRIX RABBIT NITE-LITE
by SYLVANIA
(see back of package)
General Mills ©
12.75 OZ. NET WT.

1. In a small, heavy-bottomed saucepan, melt the butter. Add the lemon juice, peel, and ½ cup sugar. Stir to mix well.

2. In a small mixing bowl, combine the egg yolks and whole egg and beat well. Beat about ½ cup of the hot mixture into the egg mixture, then return to the pan. Cook over medium heat, stirring constantly, until the mixture has thickened. Do not allow to come to a boil. Remove from the heat and cool, stirring occasionally. Cover and chill at least 1 hour.

CREAM TOPPING

1 cup heavy cream, whipped

TO ASSEMBLE

Lightly crush 12 to 14 cookies. Place about ¼ cup broken cookies in the bottom of each of 4 wine goblets or martini glasses. Spoon 2 tablespoons of the lemon mixture over the cookie layer then add a layer of whipped cream. Repeat the layers. Top each dessert with one whole cookie.

Serves 4

Raspberry Red, Lemon Yellow, Orange Orange . . .

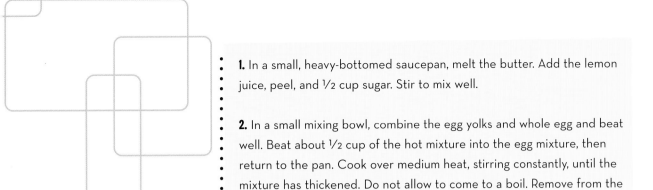

THE *Goodness* OF FRUIT FLAVOR CORN PUFFS

BL (FRIED GREEN) T SALAD
WITH CREAMY BASIL DRESSING

SALAD
. . . . .

8 slices thick-cut bacon

1/2 cup all-purpose flour

2 eggs, lightly beaten

2 cups lightly crushed Kix (they should appear flaky;
    about 2 1/3 cups uncrushed)

8 slices green tomato, 1/4 inch thick

1 cup olive oil

Salt and black pepper

6 cups baby arugula

1. Preheat the oven to 350 degrees.

2. Arrange the bacon slices in a single layer on a rimmed baking sheet.
Bake until crisp, about 15 minutes. Transfer to paper towels to drain.
Reduce the oven temperature to 200 degrees.

3. Place the flour on a small plate. Place the eggs in a small bowl. Place
the crushed Kix in a pie plate or dinner plate.

4. Working with 1 tomato slice at a time, coat with flour, dip in egg, then
press into Kix, turning to coat both sides. Transfer to a baking sheet or
tray. Line another baking sheet with paper towels.

5. Heat the oil in a large, heavy skillet over medium-high heat. Working in
batches, fry a few tomatoes at a time, just until golden, about 2 minutes
per side. Remove with a slotted spoon to the prepared baking sheet. Season to taste with salt and pepper. Keep them warm in the oven while frying the remaining tomatoes.

CREAMY BASIL DRESSING

½ cup packed fresh basil leaves

1 tablespoon chopped shallot

¼ cup olive oil

3 tablespoons mayonnaise

2 tablespoons white wine vinegar

1 tablespoon Dijon mustard

Salt and black pepper

In a blender, combine the basil, shallot, oil, mayonnaise, vinegar, and mustard. Process to blend. Season to taste with salt and pepper.

TO ASSEMBLE

Divide the arugula equally among 4 dinner plates. Arrange 2 tomato slices over each salad. Drizzle the dressing over the tomatoes, allowing some to spill onto the arugula. Top each salad with 2 bacon slices, crumbling them, if desired.

Serves 4

*Kid tested.
Mother approved.*

General G Mills
CORN
KiX®
Goodness IN CRISPY CORN PUFFS
ONE MILLION
DOLLAR OFFER
$100,000
GRAND PRIZE
SEE BACK OF PACKAGE
General Mills ©

BLACK BEAN BURGERS

Two (15-ounce) cans black beans, well drained
¼ cup chopped fresh cilantro
1 jalapeño pepper, stemmed, seeded, and minced
1 cup crushed Kix (about 2 cups uncrushed)
Salt and freshly ground black pepper
2 tablespoons vegetable oil
Prepared barbecue sauce
Hamburger buns
Lettuce leaves (optional)

1. Place half of the beans in a small bowl and mash to a smooth paste. Stir in the remaining beans along with the cilantro and jalapeño. Add 1 cup crushed Kix and stir to blend thoroughly. Form the mixture into 4 patties.

2. Place the remaining Kix on a plate. Carefully press the patties into Kix, then flip them, and repeat until coated.

3. In large skillet, heat the oil over medium heat. Carefully add the bean patties and sauté about 1 minute. Carefully turn and sauté 1 minute longer or until heated through.

4. To serve, top the patties with barbecue sauce and serve on buns with lettuce, if desired.

 Serves 4

THE *Goodness* OF CRISPY CORN PUFFS

RUM-RAISIN APPLE GALETTE

FLO BRAKER is a contributor to the *San Francisco Chronicle* and author of the beloved *Simple Art of Perfect Baking*. While she cops to the fact that more mainstream big names—Wheaties, Total, Honey Bunches of Oats, "even Raisin Bran"—could work in this recipe, her preference is for Uncle Sam, one of the cereal industry's boutique brands. "I love the idea of taking something I eat every morning and using it in a new way . . ."

We agree. Uncle Sam contains flax seeds—which not only give the crust a great texture, but a wonderful nutty flavor.

PASTRY

⅓ cup Uncle Sam cereal
1 cup all-purpose flour
2 teaspoons sugar
¼ teaspoon salt
½ cup (8 tablespoons) unsalted butter, cut into 6 pieces
4 tablespoons ice water

1. In a food processor, pulse the cereal, flour, sugar, and salt until the cereal almost disappears. Lift the lid and scatter the chunks of butter over the flour mixture; pulse the mixture until it resembles a very coarse meal with the butter smaller yet chunky. Add the ice water, a tablespoon at a time, and pulse with each addition just until combined (do not let the dough form a ball).

2. Gently press the mixture together on a sheet of plastic wrap into a 5-inch round; cover securely and refrigerate for at least 2 hours or up to 2 days.

FILLING

· · · · ·

½ cup golden raisins

1 tablespoon plus ½ teaspoon dark rum or orange juice

1 tablespoon all-purpose flour

¼ cup (4 tablespoons) sugar

2 teaspoons finely grated lemon (or orange) zest

½ teaspoon ground cinnamon

¼ teaspoon ground allspice

3 medium (each about 7 ounces) Golden Delicious apples, peeled, cored, halved, and sliced ⅛ inch thick to yield 4½ cups

2 tablespoons unsalted butter, melted

½ teaspoon dark rum

1. Adjust the rack to the lower third of the oven then preheat oven at least 20 minutes to 400 degrees.

2. In a small bowl, blend the raisins with 1 tablespoon of the rum; set aside. In a large bowl, whisk or stir together the flour, sugar, lemon zest, cinnamon, and allspice. Add the apples and toss to coat. Add the remaining ½ teaspoon of rum to the melted butter, and pour over apple slices; add the raisins with any liquid. Toss again.

TO ASSEMBLE

· · · · · · · · ·

1. Flour the work surface. Unwrap the dough and roll it into a circle about 14 inches in diameter and ⅛ inch thick. Drape the dough over the rolling pin and transfer it to a parchment-lined baking sheet.

2. Scatter the apple mixture evenly over the pastry, leaving a 2¼-inch border around the edge. Gently fold this uncovered border over the apple filling, forming a strip about 2 inches wide around the circumference of the galette and leaving a wide opening in the center. Dip a pastry brush in water and lightly coat the pastry's edge. Sprinkle the pastry's edge with 1 to 2 teaspoons of sugar.

3. Bake 50 to 55 minutes or until the pastry is light golden in color and crisp. Remove the galette on its baking sheet to a cooling rack for 10 minutes. Slip a wide spatula (or a small baking sheet without sides) under the galette and transfer it (without the paper) to a rack. Serve warm or at room temperature the same day it is baked.

 Serves 8

FROSTED BANANA PANCAKES

Tony the Tiger made his debut in 1952 as part of a plan for a series of animal illustrations appearing on boxes of Sugar Frosted Flakes. Other animals were to include Katie the Kangaroo, Elmo the Elephant, and Newt the Gnu. Supposedly Kellogg's goal was to have a character for every letter of the alphabet, but only Tony and Katie ever made it onto the box. Thanks to a catchy slogan ("I'm here to proudly state, Sugar Frosted Flakes are gr-r-reat!"), Tony grabbed the spotlight, and Katie, along with the others, quickly faded into advertising history.

1 cup all-purpose flour

1 cup ground Frosted Flakes (about 3 cups uncrushed)

1 teaspoon baking powder

½ teaspoon baking soda

¼ teaspoon salt

2 eggs, lightly beaten

1 cup mashed ripe bananas (about 2 large)

1 cup buttermilk

½ teaspoon vanilla extract

Vegetable oil

Sliced bananas, powdered sugar, and/or maple syrup

Those big crisp flakes of corn with that secret toasted-in sugar frosting

WELCOME TO
Kellogg's
of
BATTLE CREEK

Tony the Tiger was originally designed by Martin Provensen, a successful author and illustrator of children's books whose 1984 *The Glorious Flight: Across the Channel with Louis Blæriot* was awarded the Caldecott Medal.

1. In a large bowl, mix the flour, ground cereal, baking powder, baking soda, and salt.

2. In another bowl beat the eggs with the bananas, buttermilk, and vanilla. Add to the flour mixture and stir to blend.

3. For each pancake, pour about ⅓ cup batter onto a hot oiled griddle set over medium-high heat. Cook until the top is covered with bubbles and the edges look dry. Turn and cook on the other side.

4. Serve topped with sliced bananas and sprinkled with powdered sugar or with maple syrup.

☞ **Makes about 12 pancakes**

General **&** Mills

Cinnamon Toast Crunch

A sweetened cereal with homemade Cinnamon Toast taste!

™

NET WT 14 OZ
(396 grams)

CINNAMON TOAST CRUNCH ICE CREAM

What Trix, Lucky Charms, and Cap'n Crunch were to the sixties, and Freakies and the "Monster Cereals" were to the seventies, Cinnamon Toast Crunch was to the eighties—the cereal that defined a decade. It was introduced in 1984, and the first generation of kids reared on it are now of college age, which probably explains why at the University of La Verne in La Verne, California, a key complaint students had in a 2002 survey regarding the cafeteria was that Cinnamon Toast Crunch was consistently unavailable. School officials, sensing potential unrest on their hands, quickly took action—and awarded the food service contract to a new provider.

Many colleges now allow students the opportunity to vote on what cereals they want offered in their dining facilities, and ranking number one (hanging chads be damned) for the last three years at the University of Minnesota, at the University of Wisconsin, and at the University of Georgia (just to name a few) is Cinnamon Toast Crunch.

The people have spoken.

2 cups heavy cream
2 cups half and half
Four 3-inch cinnamon sticks, broken in pieces
1/2 vanilla bean, split lengthwise
8 egg yolks
3/4 cup sugar
1 cup lightly crushed Cinnamon Toast Crunch (about 1 1/2 cups uncrushed)
2 tablespoons melted butter
1 tablespoon maple syrup

1. In a heavy saucepan, combine the heavy cream and the half and half. Add the cinnamon. Scrape the seeds from the vanilla bean into the mixture and then add the pod. Set over medium heat and bring just to a boil.

2. In a medium bowl, whisk the yolks and sugar. Whisk about 1 cup hot cream mixture into the yolks, then return the mixture to the pan. Cook over low heat, stirring constantly, just until the mixture begins to thicken, about 7 minutes. Transfer to a bowl, cover, and chill at least 8 hours or overnight.

3. Meanwhile, preheat the oven to 200 degrees.

4. In a bowl, combine crushed cereal, butter, and syrup, and toss to mix thoroughly. Spread on a foil-lined baking sheet and place in the oven 4 minutes. Cool, then break into small pieces.

5. Strain the chilled custard into the container of an ice cream maker and freeze according to the manufacturer's directions. Add the cereal pieces and turn several times just to fold in.

6. Pack the ice cream into the freezer storage container and freeze until ready to serve.

☞ **Makes about 1 quart**

LUCKY CHARMED UTAH LAMB

In April 2004, among the top local culinary stars challenged by *Salt Lake* magazine to create a dish using lamb, leeks, and Lucky Charms was **DAVID JONES**, executive chef and owner of Log Haven Restaurant. Combining nouvelle flair and mind-boggling creativity, Jones concocted a recipe for an incredible Morgan Valley Lamb tenderloin (with mushroom duxelles) which he roasted inside a leek, then served with a Malbec wine demiglace and a Lucky Charms Marbits-infused balsamic syrup—and a salad of baby spinach garnished with toasted Lucky Charms oats on the side. The results were so interesting and luscious that it had critics wishing it would make is way onto the restaurant's menu so everyone could try it.

Again, this dish takes some work—not to mention patience, concentration, know-how, and a deft hand in the kitchen. To help, Jones has broken it down into six major steps and even offers these shortcuts to ease the load: (1) You can make the duxelles, the Malbec wine sauce, and the balsamic syrup a day or two in advance and refrigerate until needed. (2) If you want to utilize the Lucky Charms cooking concept but bypass the lamb-leek-mushrooms combo altogether, fix the sauce and the syrup, and then use them with any primal cut of steak, lamb, chops, or poultry.

Either way, you'll agree: it's "magically delicious."

MUSHROOM DUXELLES

8 shallots, diced
2 tablespoons olive oil
1½ pounds mushrooms, pureed
3 tablespoons reduced chicken stock
3 tablespoons fresh chopped parsley
1 tablespoon fresh chopped thyme
1 cup dry white wine
Salt and black pepper to taste

Sweat the shallots in the olive oil until translucent, then add the mushroom puree and sauté on medium-high approximately 10 minutes, constantly stirring. Add the chicken stock, parsley, thyme, and wine; reduce heat, and continue to sauté until the liquid cooks out (approximately 20 to 25 minutes). Refrigerate until needed.

LAMB TENDERLOINS IN LEEK TUBES

2 to 2½ pounds lamb
Salt and black pepper
Olive oil
6 leeks

1. Cut off the tapered ends of the lamb so it will be more uniform in shape, then cut into 6 pieces, 5 to 6 ounces each. Season with the salt and pepper. Using a little olive oil, sear the loins in a hot sauté pan. Reserve and refrigerate until needed for assembly.

2. Cut the white portion of the leek down to approximately 3½ to 4 inches. Blanch them in salted water for 30 to 40 seconds, then remove and immediately plunge them into an ice bath. Remove most of the inner core, creating a tube. Set aside.

MALBEC WINE REDUCTION

¼ cup diced shallots
2 garlic cloves, crushed
½ tip peppercorn, crushed
1 tablespoon mustard seeds, toasted
5 sprigs fresh thyme
2 sprigs fresh rosemary
½ bunch parsley stems
2 whole bay leaves
2 cups demiglace (reduced veal stock)
1 cup Malbec (Gascon 2002 or a California Syrah)
1 tablespoon unsalted butter
Salt and black pepper to taste

Pink hearts, yellow moons, orange stars, green clovers . . .

1. Tie the shallots, cloves, peppercorn, mustard seeds, thyme, rosemary, parsley stems, and bay leaves in cheesecloth to make a sachet.

2. Place the sachet, demiglace, and Malbec in a saucepan at a low simmer and reduce by two-thirds (or until you can run your finger through the sauce on the back of a spoon and the line you just created remains intact; this should take about 20 minutes). Remove the sachet and finish the sauce with butter. Season with the salt and pepper, if needed. Set aside in a warm place or store refrigerated for up to 2 days. Will make about 1½ cups.

BALSAMIC SYRUP

. . . .

2/3 cup balsamic vinegar

1/3 cup Lucky Charms Marbits (marshmallow pieces)

1 teaspoon Dijon mustard

Dash of soy sauce

Freshly ground black pepper

Combine all the ingredients in a medium saucepan over a low simmer, and reduce until the liquid reaches a syrup consistency (approximately 10 to 15 minutes). Will make about 1/2 cup. Set aside until needed.

SPINACH SALAD

. . . .

1/4 cup Lucky Charms oats

5 tablespoons extra-virgin olive oil

1 tablespoon lemon juice

1 small shallot, diced

Pinch of sugar

Salt and black pepper, to taste

11/2 to 2 cups baby spinach leaves

3 strips thinly cut bacon, cooked and crumbled

1. Preheat the oven to 350 degrees.

2. Toss the Lucky Charms oats in 1 tablespoon of the olive oil, then place in a baking pan in the oven for approximately 3 to 4 minutes, or until slightly toasted.

3. In a small bowl, mix together the remaining olive oil, lemon juice, shallot, sugar, salt, and pepper. Toss with the spinach and bacon, and garnish with the toasted Lucky Charms. Set aside.

TO FINISH

1. Preheat the oven to 450 degrees.

2. Evenly spread about 3 ounces of the mushroom duxelles over a piece of buttered $4\frac{1}{2} \times 5\frac{1}{2}$-inch plastic wrap. Place a lamb tenderloin in the center, on top of the mushrooms, then roll the wrap into a cylinder small enough to fit into the leek tube. Leave the plastic wrap open at both ends. When you have the lamb tenderloin/duxelle inside the leek, simply pull the plastic from either end so it wiggles out, but the lamb and duxelle stay put. Season the leek with a splash of olive oil, salt, and pepper, then repeat the process for each of the remaining 5 leeks.

3. Place the 6 lamb-stuffed leeks in a baking dish and roast approximately 7 to 10 minutes. Once done, allow the leeks to rest for 10 minutes.

TO ASSEMBLE

Place the lamb-leek diagonally across center of the plate. On the lower side of it, spoon a ¼ cup (4 tablespoons) pool of sauce. Around the high end of the leek (and running to the center of the top of the plate), distribute 4 teaspoons of syrup, in a dot or squiggle pattern, if desired. Fill the empty area with a small serving of spinach salad.

 **Makes 6 servings**

The technical (copyrighted) name for the mini marshmallows found in Lucky Charms (and other breakfast cereals) are Marbits; they were invented, as was the cereal, by General Mills VP John Holahan in 1963, when he cut up a few orange marshmallow Circus Peanuts, stirred them into a bowl of Cheerios, and was impressed with what he tasted.

INDEX OF RECIPES BY CEREAL BRAND

PERMISSIONS AND CREDITS

All images of General Mills–owned products and characters used with permission of General Mills Archives. Cheerios, Trix, Kix, Lucky Charms, Cocoa Puffs, Wheaties, Cinnamon Toast Crunch, Corn Chex, Wheat Chex, Franken Berry, Fruit Brute, Kaboom, King Vitaman, the Cheerios Kid, the Trix Rabbit, L. C. Leprechaun, and Sonny are registered trademarks of General Mills. © General Mills.

All images of Kellogg's–owned products and characters used with permission of the Kellogg Co. Frosted Flakes, Rice Krispies, Cocoa Krispies, Froot Loops, Special K, Corn Pops, Sugar Pops, Apple Jacks, Kellogg's Corn Flakes, Kellogg's Raisin Bran, Tony the Tiger, Toucan Sam, Snap Crackle & Pop, and Sugar Pops Pete are registered trademarks of the Kellogg Co. © Kellogg N.A. Co.

All images of Post Cereal packages and characters are use with permission of KF Holdings. Post, Honeycomb, Alpha-Bits, Sugar Crisp, Golden Crisp, Grape Nuts, Post Shredded Wheat, Cream of Wheat, Sugar Bear, and Loveable Truly are registered trademarks of KF Holdings. © KF Holdings.

Cap'n Crunch, Life cereal, Quisp, Quake, and the Quaker Oats Man are registered trademarks of The Quaker Oats Co. © The Quaker Oats Co.

Uncle Sam and Erewhon Crispy Brown Rice are registered trademarks of U.S. Mills.

The cereal box images featured in the pages of this book are courtesy of the collection of Robb Berry and *Planet Q! The Cereal Collectors Magazine*, with the following exceptions:
Wheaties box and images courtesy of the General Mills Archives
Trix box courtesy of the General Mills Archives
Cocoa Puffs box images courtesy of the General Mills Archives
Corn Chex box images courtesy of the General Mills Archives
Cinnamon Toast Crunch box images courtesy of the General Mills Archives
Rice Krispies box images provided by the Kellogg Co.
Froot Loops box images provided by the Kellogg Co.
Sugar Pops box images provided by the Kellogg Co.
Honeycomb box images provided by KF Holdings
Shredded Wheat box image from the collection of Dan Goodsell
Cereal box paintings © 2004 Burton Morris
The Last Pancake Breakfast © 2000 Dick Detzner
Blue Man Group photo courtesy of Las Vegas News Bureau

ACKNOWLEDGMENTS

Thanks to Rick Bayless, Flo Braker, James DiStefano, Gale Gand, David Jones, Annie Miler, Martha Rose Shulman, Caprial Pence, Pilar Sanchez, Art Smith, and Sherry Yard for allowing me to use (and some might say "abuse") their good names, and for making it legit for me to include the term "gourmet" in the title.

. . . Karen Gillingham, for not only not laughing when I said things like, "Can't we put Cocoa Puffs in that?" but for never failing to figure out the perfect way to do it.

. . . Robb Berry, for his knowledge, insight, and graciousness in sharing his collection of over one thousand cereal boxes.

. . . The corporate historians and public relations departments who gave me access to their companies' archives, particularly Katie Dishman (General Mills) and Nancy Sackrider (Kellogg's).

. . . Andrews McMeel for having the good taste to say "yes" to this project—and particularly Dorothy O'Brien, for being the prize inside the box.

General Mills
JETS
Goodness IN SUGAR-TOASTE
OATS 'N WHEAT
NEW POUR'N SEAL SPOUT
SEE PACKAGE BACK
General Mills

NABISCO
RICE
HONEYS
THE ORIGINAL HONEY FLAVORED CEREA
flavored with
NATURAL
HONEY
FREE INSIDE!
Plastic Model
PRE-HISTORIC
BEAST
SEE BACK OF PACKAGE
NET WT. 8½ OZS.

c